Mountain Biking Colorado's La Platas

Mountain Biking Colorado's La Platas

Great Rides Between Durango and Telluride

Derek Ryter

Pruett Publishing Company
Boulder, Colorado

© 1995 by Derek Ryter

ALL RIGHTS RESERVED. No part of this book may be reproduced without written permission from the publisher, except in the case of brief excerpts in critical reviews and articles. Address all inquiries to: Pruett Publishing Company, 2928 Pearl Street, Boulder, Colorado 80301.

Printed in the United States
10 9 8 7 6 5 4 3 2 1

Library of Congress Cataloging-in-Publication data

Ryter, Derek.
    Mountain biking Colorado's La Platas : great rides between Durango and Telluride / by Derek Ryter.
        p.   cm.
    Includes bibliographical references and index.
    ISBN 0-87108-860-6 (pbk.)
        1. All terrain cycling—Colorado—Durango Region—Guidebooks.
2. All terrain cycling—Colorado—Telluride Region—Guidebooks.
3. Durango Region (Colorado)—Guidebooks. 4. Telluride Region (Colorado)—Guidebooks. I. Title.
GV1045.5.C62D877   1995
796.6'4—dc20   95-3520
                                                                                         CIP

Cover design by Kathy McAffrey, Cover to Cover Design
Book design by Jody Chapel, Cover to Cover Design
Cover photograph by John Gilbert

Contents

Acknowledgments	vii
Introduction	ix
Cultural History of the La Plata Mountains Area	**1**
Anasazi	1
Europeans, White Settlers, and the Ute	3
Mining	5
Cattle	6
Timber	7
Mesa Verde National Park	8
Natural History	**11**
Environment	11
Wildlife	11
Geology	13
Biking in the La Platas	**17**
Backcountry Hazards and Safety	20
Other Trail Traffic	22
West Mancos River Drainage	**23**
Transfer Campground:	**24**
Jersey Jim Loop	26
Morrison Trail 610	29
Golconda	33
North Fork	37
Windy Gap/Twin Lakes	41
Chicken Creek Trail	45
Gold Run Loop	48
Chicken Creek Road Loop	50

Transfer to Millwood	52
Haycamp Point	54

T-Down Corral: 60

Rampart Hills	61
Graybeal Spring	64
Coyote Park Loop	66
Echo Basin Loop	70
The Hogback	73
Millwood	76

East Mancos River Drainage 77

East Mancos Trails	78
Railroad Grade	80
Rush Basin	82
Madden Peak	86
Menefee Peak	88

La Plata Canyon 91

Cumberland Basin	93
Allard Mine	96
Boren Creek	98
Eagle Pass	101
Tomahawk Mine	104
Snowstorm Peak Loop	107

McPhee Reservoir 110

House Creek Area	111

Dolores River Rides 114

Bear Creek to Gold Run	115
Stoner Mesa	118

Other Rides Around Mancos 121

Weber Canyon	122

Bibliography	125
Index	127

Acknowledgments

The historical information in this book was gathered predominantly from the amazing collection of local history belonging to Fern Ellis, the author's lifelong neighbor and sometimes honorary grandparent. Her book *Come Back to My Valley* provides a snapshot and memoirs of life in and around Mancos from 1874 to 1910. Duane Smith's *Rocky Mountain Boom Town* was also used, for cultural development, though it focuses on Durango. *The Anasazi and Mesa Verde National Park* is a short book by accomplished archaeologist Gilbert Wenger, and a truly fascinating study of the climate change and its effect on the Anasazi is the published research of Ken Petersen. The history of the Anasazi and their relationship with the earth can tell us a lot about the impacts of climate and land use on our ability to live in the West.

This book was prepared from the author's knowledge and experiences, but an invaluable amount of advice and review was offered by John Gilbert and Bill and Sue Ryter. Riding companions include Jodi, Bill, Jarral, Kendal, and Ellen Ryter, and John Gilbert. And thanks to Ned Overend for the support.

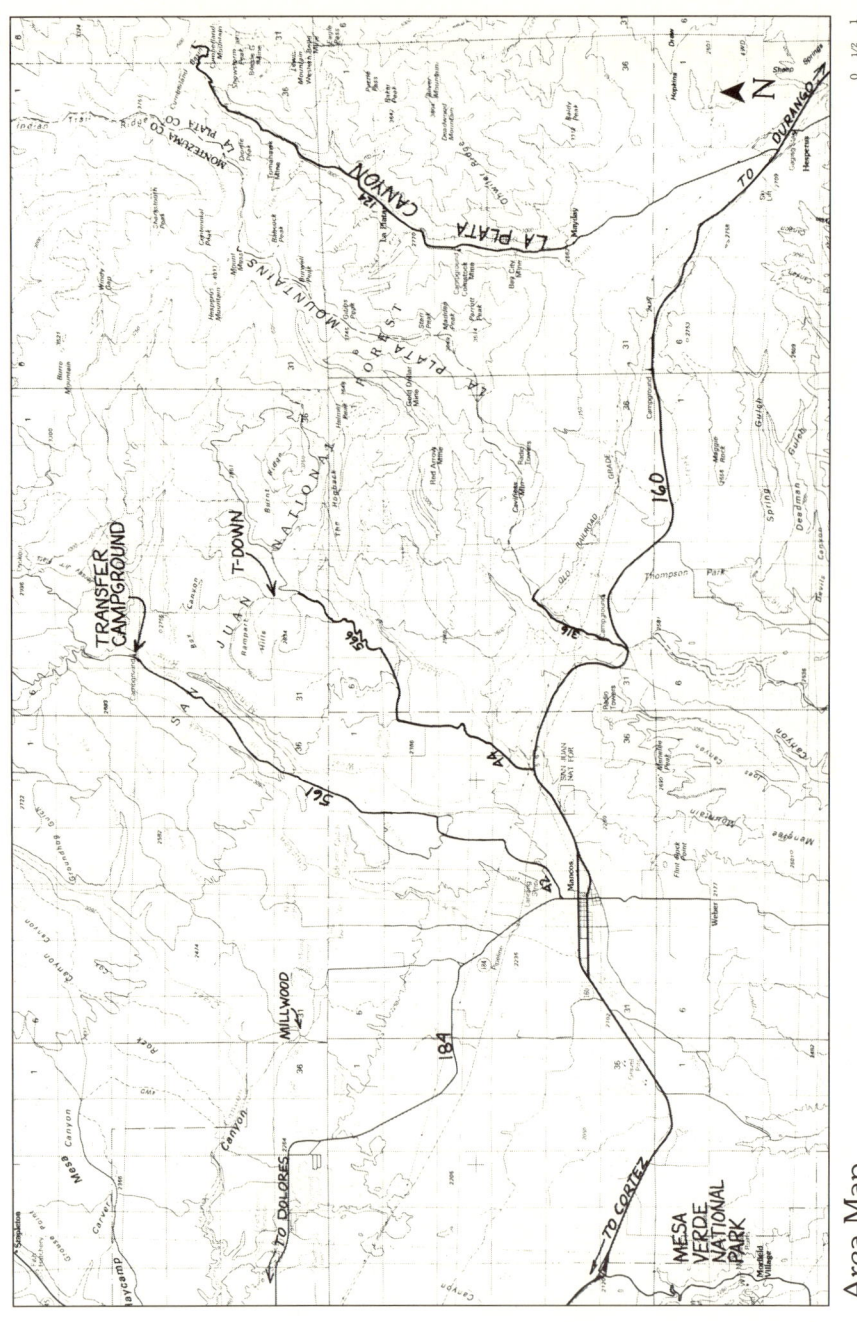

Area Map

Introduction

Just west of Durango, the La Plata Mountains are one of the best-kept mountain-bike secrets in Colorado. There are so many old logging and mining roads now closed to motorized vehicles but open to hiking and biking there that it would take several seasons to ride them all. The town of Mancos is located in the valley that bears its name at the western foot of the La Plata Mountains. This is a very scenic area that ranges from sagebrush and piñon and juniper forests to alpine environments. Mancos is reached by U.S. Highway 160 (the Navajo Trail), on part of the San Juan scenic byway, and is recommended as a jumping-off point for biking in the western La Platas. Cortez and Durango (20 miles west and 30 miles east, respectively) also offer a variety of lodging and dining accommodations. Camping is available at several Forest Service and private campgrounds in the area.

The town of Dolores is located 20 miles (32 kilometers) northwest of Mancos, via State Highway (Colorado) 184 north and Colorado 145 east. Beyond Dolores along the Dolores River is another group of trails, two of which are also described.

While providing mountain bike routes, this book also outlines the cultural and natural history of the La Plata Mountains and Mancos Valley and describes some of the conditions that one might face while mountain biking in the area. The trails section is subdivided into trails in three geographic areas separated by natural barriers and locations of good base camps. The first group of trails starts at Transfer Campground and remains north and west of the West Mancos River. Other trails in the West Mancos River drainage are on the southeast side of the rather formidable canyon and are based out of T-Down Park. The East Mancos River valley is a third group of trails that originate from different trailheads and also include a few rides that venture to the south onto Menefee Mountain. A fourth group of trails is located in La Plata Canyon to the east, and the last group of rides is a collage of rides around Mancos and in the Dolores River valley that originate in various locations.

The directions for reaching the three main trailheads are given once each for Transfer, T-Down, and La Plata Canyon. This should simplify the task of finding trailheads if a trip includes rides out of various locations.

The goal of this book is to introduce the western La Plata Mountains in a way that will allow you to look at them in a different light and see more than just trails, hills, and trees but rather environments, tilted beds of sandstone and shale, igneous intrusions, glaciated valleys, and places where people have lived and worked for centuries. The land can tell many a story if one knows how to read and understand it.

There is one other point that should be taken, and that is to respect the land on which you are riding. The local people can remember when there weren't so many out-of-state hunters and bikers, or pipelines and power lines transmitting power and gas through the hills for someone else's gain. So, as the San Juan National Forest says, *Tread lightly and leave the trails with as little impact as possible.*

The La Plata Mountains have thus far experienced relatively low impact, but without proper care, the trails could become as crowded and conflict-riddled as are the heavily used trails around Denver. Don't thrash or shred. Ride because you love to ride and have the patience to ride the switchbacks without cutting, dismount to allow hikers or horses to pass, and avoid uncontrollable speed.

There is some debate as to the environmental impact of off-road bicycles, and in some cases it is compared to that of horses. It is apparent from my experience on the trails in southwest Colorado that a properly ridden mountain bike can have less impact than a horse (and not leave piles of horse biscuits on the trail). The operative word here is *properly*. The greatest damage your bike can do to a trail takes place when you brake to the point of skidding. The damage is behind you but starts ruts in the trail and loosens the soil so that it can be blown or washed away.

It cannot be emphasized too strongly that the mountain bike can be a vehicle of little environmental impact with great health gains for the operator if it is ridden properly.

How to Use This Book

This book divides the rides in the La Plata Mountains into groups and features a header citing the distance, average round-trip time, difficulty rating, route tips, and the names of the USGS 7-1/2 minute quadrangle maps that cover each trail area. Distance is measured by bicycle computer, topographic maps, or both, and the time is based on a conservative estimate that allows for the terrain and elevation gain. The difficulty rating is a relative qualitative scale ranging from very easy to technical and extremely difficult. A technical rating applies to the roughness of the trail surface, and the difficult or moderate rating refers to the rider's overall physical exertion. Normally, a difficult rating is given due to distance and/or elevation gain. Always refer to the furnished maps and topographic profiles in the book as well as the relevant USGS topographic map to confirm or adjust the rating according to your skill level. Ratings apply only to good weather conditions and don't include things like large cow pies or having to outrun a black bear.

Route tips describe conditions of the trails or potential weather or trail-use factors, and the elevation gain cites the maximum low and high; there aren't too many trails here that go up and down a great deal.

Use all of the information listed to prepare for any ride in this book, and get familiar with your ability to climb at different elevations. And remember, if an out-and-back trail is more than you bargained for, you can always turn around.

Cultural History of the La Plata Mountains Area

Anasazi

The earliest known inhabitants of the Mancos Valley were the Anasazi, or Ancient Ones, who also inhabited the Montezuma Valley to the west and built the pueblos and cliff dwellings preserved locally at Mesa Verde National Park and the Anasazi Cultural Center. Regionally, the Anasazi ranged across southwest Colorado, northern New Mexico, northeast Arizona, and southeast Utah. It is estimated that the first Anasazi entered the Montezuma and Mancos Valleys about two thousand years before present (B.P.) as hunters and gatherers who had acquired the cultigens of beans and squash, and corn that was first grown in southern Mexico. The Anasazi gradually became stationary farmers, and between 2,000 and 1,500 B.P. they began to build pit houses and weave baskets. Thus, the Anasazi living during this period are referred to as The Basketmakers. Between 1,500 and 1,300 B.P., as their technology grew, the Anasazi began to construct above-ground pueblos and clay pottery, both of which became higher in quality and more ornate as time went on. All of the Anasazi cultures that were in existence after 1,300 B.P. are referred to as Pueblo Indians.

The Anasazi population grew rapidly for several hundred years. They cleared land; became dryland farmers; hunted mule deer, bighorn sheep, and rabbits; and grew to a population that may have been greater than the current human numbers in the area. During this period, the Anasazi traded with cultures to the south, including the Hohokam and Mogollon in Arizona, changing their ceremonial and agricultural practices as they imported new cultigens and irrigation practices. They domesticated dogs and turkeys and wove sashes from dog fur. Yucca leaves contain strong fibers, which they spun into ropes and cords for snares and bows; they tanned leather for clothing, cradle boards, and footwear; they worked flint, obsidian, and agate into arrow and spear points. There were no known enemies of the Anasazi, who as farmers would have been vulnerable to attacks by marauding raiders. During the Pueblo culture period, it has been suggested that there was some impact by wandering Shoshonean hunters who entered the area. The Anasazi flourished between 1,300 and 690 B.P. (700 and 1300 A.D.), until they suddenly—in little more than a decade—and somewhat mysteriously, completely and permanently abandoned the area.

There are three theories for the mass exodus: 1. overpopulation and intense farming, which included clearing large tracts of the piñon-juniper forest, 2. changing climate and weather patterns, including a severe twelve-year drought around 1300 A.D., and 3. the impact of Shoshonean wanderers. Most likely, all of these factors worked together. The area available for farming on the west side of the La Platas and the eastern Colorado Plateau is limited to a specific range in altitude where the yearly precipitation and growing season are adequate for growing corn, squash, and beans. During the time of the Pueblo Anasazi, conditions fluctuated constantly because rain and snowfall patterns and temperatures vary greatly on a time scale of hundreds of years. Because the elevation where corn will grow without irrigation is very sensitive to climatic changes, the Anasazi population and its distribution fluctuated with the climate.

The large population and increasingly limited agricultural production probably impelled the Anasazi to move off the comfortable mesa-top pueblos on Mesa Verde and into the cold, damp cliff dwellings. Arroyos carved up barren fields cleared of brush, piñon, and juniper, draining sporadic summer thunderstorms that were too little and too late to save crops during drought years. Presaging the modern dust bowls, croplands dried up and soil blew into the air while masonry storage bins began to become depleted. Firewood and building materials probably were also in short supply due to the clearing of the piñon-juniper forest. Though the Anasazi population had fluctuated in number between 1000 and 1200 A.D., there was a downward trend in permanent residents after the year 1200, when the arable land underwent its largest decline.

With this decrease in arable land during 1200 to a thin strip across the valley and southern Mesa Verde, pressure from Shoshonean wanderers was probably not needed to help the remaining Anasazi decide to move south, where agriculture was doing a bit better. It is believed that the Anasazi culture dispersed and mixed into other farming cultures such as the Zuni and Acoma in New Mexico and the Hopi in Arizona.

The dwellings and artifacts found in the area are accumulated from the entire span of Anasazi settlement (five hundred years of Pueblo culture alone) and are countless. No other farming societies lived in the area until it was claimed by Anglo settlers in the late 1800s, though the Ute people hunted throughout the La Platas and surrounding country as far east as the Sangre de Cristo Mountains. When riding or hiking in the area, you will most probably travel over sites where Anasazi planted crops or Utes stalked mule deer.

Europeans, White Settlers, and the Ute

The first Europeans to enter the La Plata Mountains region were Spaniards on an expedition led by the priest Father Escalante, who camped on the Mancos River in 1776. Escalante's party traveled through the area naming geographic features such as the La Plata ("Silver") Mountains, the Animas River ("River of Lost Souls") that runs through Durango, and perhaps the Mancos River. Another account of the naming of the Mancos River describes a priest by the name of Salvero, who is believed to have visited the upper West Mancos River at some point in the 1700s and to have fallen down the bank, breaking his ankle. He and his guide barely made it back to their mission in what is now New Mexico, naming the river El Rio Mancos, which has been interpreted by the Colorado State Historical Society as meaning "River of the Cripples." Navajos in the area are also said to have referred to the Mancos River as *Tow-za-leen,* for which there is no English translation.

Other white men traveled through the area, but the first to settle in the Mancos Valley were Dick Giles and John Ratliff, who were working for a man named John Moss on a prospecting expedition to the La Platas in 1874. Giles was taken by the fertile soil and rich grazing land, and he returned to the Mancos Valley in 1875 to construct the first cabin there. None of these men or any others described herein are legends in lore or nationally known explorers, but you will see their names on many peaks, canyons, springs, and lakes in the La Plata Mountains and Mancos Valley.

The town of Mancos was effectively founded when several other cabins were constructed in 1876 by cowboys George Frink, Lou Paquin, and Wylie Graybeal, who had pushed two thousand head of cattle through the valley the year before on their way to Monticello, Utah. The Menefee family moved into the valley before 1880 and built the cabin that still stands on the Reddert Ranch just north of U.S. Highway 160 on Montezuma County Road 44, 3 miles (5 kilometers) east of Mancos. The Menefees' first son was the first white boy born in the Mancos Valley. The first general store was opened by George Bauer in 1881 in a small cabin. George Bauer later started the first bank and mercantile and became the first county commissioner when Montezuma County was formed by dividing La Plata County in two in 1886. Dick Giles was killed by Utes in 1878.

Mancos grew rapidly from 1881 to 1888 as something of a hinterland to Durango, and a schoolhouse and other stores were built as the cattle business expanded. In 1881, the last of the Ute resistance was suppressed with the help of U.S. Army soldiers from Fort Lewis, which was built south of the town of Hesperus. Soon after, leaders and residents in Durango fought to move the remaining Utes completely out of the area and into Utah. To the dismay of Durangoans, the federal government redefined the Ute Nation as a fifteen-mile-wide strip of land bordered on the south by New Mexico and extending from Utah to east of Durango and including the town of Ignacio, which was named for the Ute leader. It was believed by the white folk that this area contained far too much arable land that they could cultivate much better than could the Utes. Durango's highly debated Animas–La Plata water project was developed primarily to repay the Utes for a land deal made during this time. By 1888 the soldiers from Fort Lewis were more of a market for products than they were protection from marauding aboriginals, though soldiers were later used to help suppress labor disputes in Cripple Creek and local coal mines.

The Ute people were divided into two tribes on two reservations: the Southern Utes on the east, and the Ute Mountain Utes on the west. The two reservations are separated directly south of Mancos. Much of this land is semi-arid and hilly. Wildlife thrives in this area, and there are many other large Anasazi cliff dwellings in the lower Mancos canyon. The Ute Tribe has begun plans for a tribal park there and have conducted bike tours into the canyons to view some of the unexcavated dwellings.

The Denver and Rio Grande Railroad (D&RG) extended its tracks through Mancos in 1891, and the first train made a stop there that fall. The railroad helped the growing cattle and timber industries, and mining operations that were extracting low-grade ore previously too expensive to transport to a smelter. All in all, however, the railroad helped Durango more than it did the local small towns, because the D&RG planned and developed Durango, making it the link to the mines of Silverton.

Durango's smelters, located across the Animas River from the current Durango sewage treatment plant and less than a mile south of the U.S. 160 bridge, were running at capacity during the 1890s, bringing money into the town. While smelter smoke filled the Animas Valley, the Mancos and Montezuma Valleys were becoming secondary to Durango, which was very competitive, capitalizing on every resource it could get its figurative hands on. Without a smelter or rich ore deposits, Mancos and Cortez were left to agrarian pursuits that were more stable than minerals, though much less lucrative in the short term.

Mining

The first placer gold deposits were discovered by Captain George A. Jackson in 1892 on the North Fork of the West Mancos River, upstream from what is now called Golconda, though legend has it that a gold nugget was discovered in the same area more than a century earlier by the Spanish Father Salvero. Jackson set up a placer operation on the West Mancos River, and remnants of buildings and a stamping mill are still located at what became known as Jackson City.

The first stamping mill was built by John Wade and J. M. Rush using stream water from the East Mancos River to power the North Star Mine, located in what is now Rush Basin. Stamping mills would crush the ore, then mercury would be mixed into attract free gold. The Doyle Mine in Rush Basin had the highest yield and longest production life in the area until, in the winter of 1936, a huge avalanche swept virtually all of its buildings and six people down into the canyon.

There were many mine prospects and endless speculation in the La Plata Mountains during the late 1880s, and the towns of Mancos, La Plata, Parrott City, Cortez, and Dolores grew because of it. A large deposit was never found, however, and mining declined for the most part by the 1930s. Several mines (for instance the Bessie G and Columbus Basin Mines) are still in operation in La Plata Canyon and on the east side of the mountains. The Forest Service is currently working to restore the West Mancos River fish habitat in places where placer mining has virtually wiped out the valley bottom.

Coal mining was also very active in the area, starting around 1900 with the expansion of mineral exploration and timber cutting combined with the continued growth of the cattle business. The Menefee family pioneered coal mining in the hills south of the La Platas, some of which would later be named for the family: Menefee Mountain and Menefee Peak. They found relatively rich though thin seams of coal in the Cretaceous Mesa Verde Group between beds of sandstone and shale. This geological unit was also named after the family as the Menefee Formation of the Mesa Verde Group. Coal mines can be seen on rides south of Mancos Hill to Menefee Peak, and the radio towers may be seen on the east side of East Canyon.

The mining history of the La Platas was never anything special, and after the silver crash in 1893 that sank even the large mines in Silverton and Telluride, it was evident that mines that could not produce large quantities of gold were doomed to fail. Other industries, such as lumber, made their mark, but cattle was destined to be the breadwinner for the Mancos Valley.

Cattle

The cattle industry was active in the area even before the town of Mancos was built, and the first cabins were built by cattlemen. As it turned out, the cattle and farming industries persevered far beyond the time that mining and timber were profitable. In the local area, cattle is still a commodity, and bikers and motorists alike may get caught behind a herd being moved by cowboys either up or down (into or out of the mountains), depending on the season.

The aspen forests provide grazing for the bovines in the summer months, which is why you might see one or more on the trails, and in the autumn ranchers will bring the cattle down to the valleys to winter on fields that were used during summer to grow hay. Thanks to irrigation canals and reservoirs, the amount of land that can be used to raise cattle has remained relatively constant through changing rainfall patterns. The Anasazi had limited technology which forced them to adapt by migrating.

Timber

Also associated with the growth of mining, cattle, and construction in Mancos, Cortez, and Dolores, logging became big business in the La Platas. In the early 1880s, J. M. Rush of mining fame started a lumber mill in Mancos, and Major E. C. Cooper started one in Parrott City, located in La Plata Canyon. Logging was extensive in the thick stands of high-yield Douglas fir and Engelmann spruce blanketing the La Plata Mountains, with equally profitable stands of pine on the foothills and Menefee Mountain. There was, however, no forest management; cutting was indiscriminate, and loggers did not control the waste wood (slash) that was trimmed off of timber in the field and at mill sites.

Because of the lack of effective management, most of the timber in the forests that you will see in the area is at least second growth, and only the trees in inaccessible areas such as the top of Menefee Mountain or in Lost Canyon might be old growth. A large forest fire also raged through the forest north of Millwood in 1900, and it was most likely facilitated by the slash wood left on the forest floor. The actual extent of the burn is not known, but there are many places on Haycamp Mesa between Lost Canyon and Chicken Creek Canyon where burned stumps can still be seen.

The first large lumber mill was built on the route from Transfer Campground to Windy Gap and Gold Run in the area that is now named for it: Spruce Mill Park. Many other mills were built (eight were in operation in 1907), and many made good money, though nearly every timber operation had to deal with fires that wiped out the mills at one time or another. Some mill owners rebuilt after fires, and others changed venues. When the railroad was built in 1891, there was so much lumber production that the D&RG built a spur track north to Millwood, then on west down Lost Canyon. Millwood is now little more than some old roadbeds in the woods west of Joe Moore Reservoir. The Millwood Junction Restaurant in Mancos is named after that old rail stop.

The first forest management in the area was undertaken in 1908, when the Montezuma National Forest was established (the office was located in Mancos). The timber industry peaked about the same time, however, as mining and construction quickly leveled off. Local logging associated with lumber production persists only at the top of Mancos

Hill at Ott's Mill, possibly the last small-scale operation that will ever exist in the area. On a larger scale, the Ohio Blue Tip Match Company operated a matchstick factory at the west end of Mancos until the mid 1980s. The company was one of the largest producers of matchsticks in the country. This plant now logs aspen trees from the La Plata Mountains for Western Timber, which runs an excelsior plant.

Although limited mining also persists, predominantly at the Red Arrow Mine on the East Mancos River, the demand on the forest has shifted markedly in the last ten years from a resource-extraction base to a real estate and recreational base. This is illustrated in East Canyon, where it is indeed ironic that coal mines look down on the recent real estate development of Elk Springs Ranch, which is not a true ranch but a collection of residents who have moved to the area from California. It should also be noted that recreation has been a part of the Mancos Valley and the La Platas as far back as 1898, when the Kelly and Jarrett Livery and Feed in Mancos began outfitting tourists to visit the Anasazi cliff dwellings on Mesa Verde by horseback.

Mesa Verde National Park

The discovery of Anasazi cliff dwellings on Mesa Verde in 1888 by the Wetherills of Mancos immediately stimulated interest among locals and tourists. When discovered, the abandoned cliff dwellings were nothing more than piles of building stones and timbers preserved in the dry overhangs of sandstone, but they were seen by local entrepreneurs as an economic boon. It was not long before a wagon road was cut into the mesa and tours were sold. Visitors would rummage through the piles of rock, sometimes even using dynamite to excavate the sites to retrieve pots, tools, garments, human remains, and other artifacts to take home or sell. In Durango, artifacts became big business, and tourism was enthusiastically promoted; it is estimated that as many as one thousand artifacts were taken from sites in March of 1889 alone. Unfortunately, the remains of the Anasazi were also curios, and the corpse of a woman entombed in a dry room, literally mummified from lack of moisture, was exhumed and included in a parade in Durango to promote tours. This or a similar mummy was displayed at the park museum until the 1970s, when it was removed to spare the indignation of modern Native Americans.

There was opposition to the pilfering going on at the dwellings, but it was predominantly, if not exclusively, from the women of Durango. Their political influence was less than immediately effective, but after ten years of fighting, some of which had been carried on by the Colorado Federation of Women's Clubs, the fate of the dwellings was sealed: in 1906 President Theodore Roosevelt signed Mesa Verde National Park into existence, protecting the Anasazi artifacts so that archaeologists could try to unravel the history of the lost culture. The propreservation group later became the Colorado Cliff Dwellings Association.

The main office for the park was initially located in Mancos, and the town profited from tours and construction in the park. The bulk of the tours were, however, based in Durango because of the well-established large hotels and restaurants there. The park headquarters were eventually moved from Mancos to the mesa in 1937.

If you visit the park in summer months, there are roads that are open to bicycles, though no off-roading is allowed. The highway from U.S. 160 to the museum is more than 20 miles (32 kilometers) and 2,000 feet (610 meters) of elevation change, but there are other routes inside the park that are much easier.

Natural History

Environment

There are four distinct biozones in the highly variable elevation of the La Plata Mountains. The highest zone is alpine tundra, consisting of grasses and shrubs above 11,000 feet (3,353 meters) elevation. The subalpine forest between 11,000 and 9,500 feet (3,353 and 2,900 meters) consists of Engelmann spruce, Douglas fir, various shrubs and grasses, and krummholz near the upper limit (timberline). Below the subalpine, the montane zone extends from 9,500 to 7,600 feet (2,900 to 2,316 meters), and is dominated by conifers and aspens with some scrub oak. The foothills are the fourth zone, which is divided into two subzones: the upper is dominated by ponderosa and scrub oak from 7,600 to 6,500 feet (2,316 to 1,981 meters), and the lower is dominated by piñon pine and juniper below 1,228 feet (1,981 meters). Sagebrush is common in the lower foothills but can also occur at higher elevations if water is available.

The elevations of these zones are approximate, depending on slope aspect and type of soil. The zones themselves have also changed elevation in the past several thousand years, and of course did not exist as we know them during the last glacial advance.

Wildlife

Wildlife of the La Plata Mountains and Mancos Valley was plentiful when the first white men set foot in the area. This included black and some grizzly bears that are known to have roamed the San Juan Mountains to the east; elk, mule deer, bighorn sheep, mountain lions, wolves, coyotes, eagles, and red-tailed hawks; not to mention a plethora of smaller creatures such as wild turkeys, migrating waterfowl (herons, ducks, and geese), and small roosting birds and songbirds. The bighorn sheep were hunted out of the area for the most part, though efforts are currently being undertaken to reintroduce them (and are doing very well). The grizzly bear and wolf were killed across the state, and mountain lions were hunted extensively.

The grizzly has not returned (there is some debate as to whether there might be grizzly bears in the San Juan Mountains), but the black bear has flourished through hunting and habitat changes over the years, and individuals can be encountered in any part of the La Plata Mountains or Menefee Mountain. The mountain lion has increased in the area recently, partly due to the safe habitat to the west in Mesa Verde National Park and the rough and wild country on Menefee Mountain and in the Southern Ute and Ute Mountain Ute reservations to the south. Every year the debate continues about how to manage the mountain lion as its population increases and more and more discover what an easy meal a domestic sheep is.

Though the mule deer and elk numbers have decreased at different times since settlement due to habitat changes, they are common in the area, and hunters come from all over to pursue them in the late summer and fall. Care should be taken on the highways in Colorado not only because of the hunters but because deer and elk are always near roads and can cause severe damage to a car or truck.

It is very rare for a hiker or cyclist to be injured by wild animals in this part of the country, but there is always a chance that you could come up on a sow black bear with cubs or a mountain lion who for some reason decides that you are interesting enough to try to dine on. Bears are not typically hunters of big game and would much rather chew on berries or termites than try and wrestle down a human, but a sow with a cub will attack anything that appears to be a threat to her cubs. The rule of thumb when near a bear is not to approach or act threatening in any way. If attacked, assume the fetal position and remain still. Mountain lions are different animals. If you travel much in the backcountry, there is a good chance a big cat watched you ride by but just sat there twitching its tail while you remained completely unaware. Lions rarely attack humans, but if one appears to be stalking you, move away and avoid eye contact. Odds are that it will decide you are much more work than a rabbit, a fawn, or the sheep down the road.

There are also rattlesnakes in the foothills of the La Platas, and they become more common with lower elevation. The snakes are prairie rattlers growing to as long as thirty-six inches, and they are very poisonous. Fortunately, there aren't enough rattlers around to affect the average backcountry traveler, and a little caution when stepping over large rocks or logs will suffice to avoid them. The infamous jackalope has never been seen in the La Plata Mountains.

Geology

The La Plata Mountains area is interesting geologically in that it is near the boundary between the Rocky Mountain physiographic province to the east and the Colorado Plateau to the west. This affords a variety of geologic settings, and with the large elevation changes, a variety of surficial processes. Most of the area is underlain by Cretaceous sedimentary rocks of the Mesa Verde Group, Mancos Shale, Dakota Sandstone, and Morrison Formation. Regionally, these rocks all dip (slope downward) to the south, as can be seen when looking west from the La Platas toward Mesa Verde. Mesa Verde is a large *cuesta* (a ridge formed by the erosion of gently dipping erosion-resistant beds). At the foot of the La Plata Mountains, the sedimentary rocks lap up onto the intrusive core and dip off to the southwest. To the south, sediments plunge, and the Mesa Verde Group is deep underground in the San Juan Basin in northern New Mexico.

Fossils found in southwest Colorado are limited to the teeth of Cretaceous sharks that wash out of the Mancos Shale and trace fossils in the Mesa Verde Group. In sandstone beds, ripple marks and the tracks of worms and burrowing beach animals can be seen. Unfortunately, the usually rich Morrison Formation does not yield dinosaur remains like those found in northwestern Colorado.

Between the towns of Dolores and Mancos and west of the La Platas, the Mesa Verde Group and the Mancos Shale is eroded away, and the Dakota Sandstone caps the interfluves between rivers (for instance, the Dolores and Mancos Rivers), draining the La Plata Mountains. Below the Dakota Sandstone is the Morrison Formation, which forms slopes all along the rivers north of Mancos. Most of the areas described in this book are underlain by the Dakota Sandstone and Morrison Formation, with sporadic occurrences of the shallow intrusive rocks of the La Plata Mountains' igneous center.

The La Plata Mountains are of a geologic style common on the Colorado Plateau (for instance, La Sal, Abajo, or Henry Mountains) and characterized by laccolithic intrusions of magma that have pushed up and squeezed into cracks in the sedimentary rocks. Erosion then removed the less-resistant sedimentary rocks to expose the igneous core. Many of the peaks are composed of shallow intrusive rocks that cooled relatively quickly because of their shallow depth in comparison to the Pikes Peak Granite seen near Colorado Springs, which is much coarser-grained (larger crystals) due to a much slower cooling rate. Peaks such as Hesperus Mountain and Centennial Peak are banded, indicating that they are composed of uplifted sedimentary rocks, whereas the jagged peaks such as Diorite or Spiller are composed of igneous rocks riddled with vertical cooling fractures. Other features, including the Hogback, Burnt Ridge, Burro Mountain, and the Rampart Hills, are also supported by intrusives.

Igneous rocks along trails in this book are typically in the form of either sill-like masses formed by magma squeezing between beds of sedimentary rocks and producing the picturesque cliffs along the West Mancos River and Rampart Hills, or stocklike masses such as the Hogback. Igneous rock is typically a diorite, monzonite, or syenite porphyry (a fine-grained igneous rock with conspicuous crystals). These three rock types are siliceous quartz-bearing rocks (though they contain less than 20 percent quartz overall), differentiated by their ratios of alkali feldspar and plagioclase. The feldspar in syenite is between 100 percent and 66 percent alkali feldspar; monzonite is between 66 percent and 33 percent alkali feldspar; diorite is between 100 percent and 66 percent plagioclase. They are all greenish gray, light brown, gray, or grayish pink. The Audubon Society, among others, publishes field guides to rocks and minerals if you are interested in identifying individual rock specimens more precisely.

As igneous intrusions pushed through fractures and uplifted the sedimentary rocks during the Tertiary period between 80 and 30 million years ago, they brought with them hydrothermal fluids that migrated into fractures. These fluids transported minerals and elements into the rock such as iron, magnesium, copper, lead, and of course silver and gold. The gold emplaced in overlying rocks was in some cases pure, and several historical reports indicate nuggets were found in the West Mancos River. Recoverable deposits are limited, and most of the economic minerals were extracted by the 1920s.

The uplifting of the La Plata Mountains occurred during the Tertiary period, but much of the landscape seen in the high country is much younger and formed by glaciers and glacial outwash over the last one hundred thousand years, with the last glacial advance peaking around thirty thousand years ago and waning around twelve thousand years ago. Glaciers in the La Platas were limited to areas above about 8,000 feet (2,440 meters), and accumulating above 11,000 feet (3,350 meters). Most of the alpine landforms are products of weathering and erosion during and after glacial episodes. Some of the most prominent features are the large talus slopes and deposits at the bases of peaks and canyon walls. Glacial cirques such as Slide Rock, Owen, or Rush Basins are also common in the highest reaches of drainages.

Large boulder accumulations high in the La Platas with steep fronts and ridges on the surfaces are rock glaciers. In Slide Rock Basin, on the north side of Hesperus Mountain, is a good example of an active rock glacier with its steep, fresh face and sharp break with the surface caused by the whole mass moving downslope and rock toppling over the front.

Biking in the La Platas

Bicycling in Durango first became popular back in 1894, and a bicycle track (six laps per mile) was constructed as part of a parks development program. Cyclists were a bit too enthusiastic, however, and ordinances were written to calm things down; a cyclist—or at least a man on a bike—was arrested for riding down Main Street without a headlamp. Cycling back then was quite different than it is today, and not only because titanium alloys were not available. Women were not encouraged to ride because it might expose too much skin during

The Durango Wheel Club at Baker's Bridge, 1895 (photo courtesy of John Hughes).

that very conservative Victorian era; when riding with a man, the woman was to stay to the rear. What would they say if they could see Julie Furtado riding across town? The biking legacy of Durango continues—it is the home of some of the best cyclists in the world, and it's one of the best places to train as well.

For travelers to the La Plata Mountains, lodging is available in Mancos, Cortez, Durango, Dolores, or the Echo Basin Ranch east of Mancos. Camping areas are plentiful in the San Juan National Forest, though campgrounds are few in number, with local campgrounds limited to Transfer, Kroeger, and Joe Moore Reservoir. Mesa Verde National Park also offers lodging and camping.

The rides described in this book range in the technical ability and time required—from relatively easy tours to difficult and grueling full-day affairs. Thus, a cyclist at virtually any ability level will find good routes among those included here. Many of the rides involve a good deal of elevation gain, and are all above 7,000 feet (2,133 meters) in elevation at some point. Distances and elevations are approximate and err on the conservative side, and times are estimated for a cyclist who is not in a hurry, so don't be surprised if you can finish the ride below the minimum of the range provided.

All trails in the mountains begin at better than 7,000 feet (2,133 meters), so if you are not acclimated to the elevation, take it easy on your first few rides or plan for a little extra time and water. The rides chosen for this book are also for the most part restricted to closed or open four-wheel-drive roads because there are so many of them, and many of the hiking trails in the area are not always well enough maintained for bike travel. Because of the elevation gain, trails in La Plata Canyon and the upper reaches of the West Mancos River are grueling and only recommended for experienced cyclists in very good shape who are acclimated to the elevation and are ready for a serious workout. Reaching the tops of one of these rides promises a view of expanses that include lands in northern New Mexico, northeastern Arizona, and southeast Utah, not to mention the San Juan Mountains to the north and northeast.

The western La Plata Mountains and foothills offer some of the best year-round off-road cycling anywhere. The foothills are gently sloping beds of Dakota Sandstone that support broad mesalike areas that range from 7,000 to 9,500 feet (2,130 to 2,895 meters) elevation. The different branches and tributaries of the Mancos and Dolores Rivers dissect the Dakota Sandstone, creating mesa topography with steep-walled valleys and canyons. The United States Geological Survey (USGS) 7-1/2-minute topographic quadrangles (1:24,000) that cover the area in this book are: Boggy Draw, Dolores East, Hesperus, La Plata, Mancos, Millwood, Orphan Butte, Rampart Hills, Stoner, Thompson Park, and Wallace Ranch. USGS topographic county map series maps (1:50,000) are also handy for this area, with many of the trails covered by the Montezuma County Map #2 and #4, and the La Plata County Map #2. USGS 30-by-60-minute sheets (1:100,000) are available at a smaller scale in metric measurements, and the USGS and the Bureau of Land Management (BLM) together publish the Cortez 1-by-2-degree sheets that show the entire area covered here at a 1:250,000 scale. The San Juan National Forest map is available at ranger stations and mountaineering shops, and it locates some of the trails and roads better than the USGS maps do, though there is no topography and the scale is one inch equals two miles.

Mountain biking in the La Plata Mountains is similar to cycling in many other mountainous regions, though the opportunities are extraordinary here because of the many roads that were cut through the forest during the mining and logging days. Timber harvests are declining, but aspens are still taken for use in the Mancos excelsior plant, so watch for logging trucks on back roads. Many of these roads are closed to motorized vehicles due to landslides and runoff erosion, but mountain bikes can still easily negotiate many of them.

Most of the trails in this book can be ridden on an entry-level mountain bike, though climbing is easier on a lighter and lower-geared, more expensive bike. High-quality shifters and other components also make a difference, but, of course, are expensive. The most important thing is to ride a reliable bike. A very cheap bike, such as those found in Wal-Mart, may well break down on you in the wrong place, while a solid, middle-of-the-line bike will normally complete the trip. The best deals for the noncompetitive cyclist in 1995 are bikes with components such as Shimano LX or STX. The type of frame you choose is up to you, and for recreational use usually affects the ride and handling more than does the frame weight or strength. The biggest concern with any quality bike is, of course, you, the motor.

The main trail concerns that should be taken into account when riding the La Platas are related to the Mancos Shale and the Morrison Formation. These two geologic units are composed predominantly of silt and clay, which, when it becomes wet, is one of the worst things your mountain bike can encounter. The Mancos Shale is left as a thin residual deposit on top of mesas supported by Dakota Sandstone and dominates the area between the Middle and West Mancos Rivers and Bear Creek. Problems associated with engineering highways on the Mancos Shale can be seen in the road leading up the side of Mesa Verde, where the slope is continually slumping, closing the road practically as an annual event. Many of the roads and trails in the western La Platas are on the shale and can be difficult riding when an afternoon thunderstorm dumps on them. This should not discourage biking in this area, however, because mud can be avoided and there are many trails and roads on a rocky or gravel base that provides ample traction in wet or dry conditions.

Backcountry Hazards and Safety

Depending on the time of year, hazards to backcountry travelers in the La Platas can range from lightning, flooding, or dehydration to hypothermia or stray bullets from hunters. For the most part, this area has a mild climate, with very wet springs from February to May, then drier weather till mid-July, when the monsoonal moisture typically initiates daily afternoon showers. After August, fall may turn into what is known as Indian summer, characterized by dry, warm weather that can last till late October. Snow can fall above 10,000 feet (3,050 meters) virtually any time and has been known to surprise hikers or hunters, and hypothermia can become a very real danger.

Lightning accompanies summer afternoon thundershowers and can be avoided by keeping to low ground off ridges or peaks when you see a dark cloud group headed your way. These clouds can pop up very quickly, forming from the mountains themselves on warm, moist air moving up from the southwest. Thunderstorms will typically form in the afternoons, so it is best to plan trips into the high country to begin in the early morning and end around noon, unless you feel like waiting out a rainstorm or on a trail somewhere and then riding back to camp through mud.

Flooding is also associated with the rain showers but is limited to the bottoms of canyons and draws. Thus, it is advisable to watch the skies and look around to get an idea of where you might be able to get to if the creek you are riding along were to suddenly rise five feet. Flooding is, however, not common, and a simple awareness of its possibility is enough to eliminate this hazard altogether.

Southwestern Colorado, as with many high-altitude areas, is notorious for causing dehydration during outdoor activities. This is primarily because of the combination of high elevation, dry air, warm temperatures, and sunny days. All of these factors increase the rate of water loss from your body, and for most all of the rides described in this book, at least two water bottles should be carried; on longer rides it may be a good idea to take along a water filter to facilitate using extra water from the numerous creeks and lakes. The amount of water you need will increase with your level of exertion, the elevation, and the temperature, so plan for it by using topographic maps and your other cycling experiences.

Hypothermia can also be a problem, but it is usually encountered when bikers are not properly prepared. Above 10,000 feet (3,050 meters), it can snow at nearly any time of year, and when a storm hits, your temperature can drop very quickly; travel can become slow and exhausting. Equipment needed to combat hypothermia is not only raingear and emergency items like matches, but also the proper bike tools so that you can keep riding. This can in many cases get you down to a lower elevation where the storm is less intense and the air is much warmer. Recommended bike tools and supplies are listed below, though many if not all are probably already on your bike.

- Pump
- First-aid kit
- Spare tube
- Tire tool
- Patch kit
- Chain tool
- Allen wrenches
- 6-inch adjustable wrench
- 10- and 14-millimeter open-ended wrenches
- Extra power bar

The most common injuries incurred while mountain biking (assuming the rider is wearing an approved helmet) are cuts, bruises, and broken bones. Although broken bones are least likely for responsible cyclists, one should be familiar with appropriate first-aid measures and methods of transporting an injured companion. Much more common are cuts and scrapes, so your first-aid kit should include bandages, antibiotic ointment, and large gauze pads.

Other Trail Traffic

The La Plata Mountains area is used heavily for cattle ranching and recreation, so other than a hiker, one of the things one might encounter on the trails is a horse or a Hereford bull or cow. It is, of course, a rule of the trail for bikers to yield to hikers or horseback riders, but there is no question one should give ample room to the Herefords, particularly because they sometimes have a shorter temper than hikers or horses. And there are times when a cow will feel her calf is in danger, so if you notice a bawling calf off to your right and a big mother cow off to your left, simply remain calm and try to ride to a spot that is not between the two.

Some trails are especially popular for horseback riding, and there are stretches of trail that are steep with limited visibility. Because of this, extra care should be given to speed on descents and through winding trails to avoid meeting a horse while traveling at an uncontrollable rate. As stated previously, trails with heavy horse traffic are in worse condition than are trails that do not see the horses, with more ruts, exposed roots, and rocks, and thus more unrideable or technical sections, so extra care should be taken on them.

It should also be noted that four-wheel-drives and ATVs also use some of these roads, and it is best to use caution and ride defensively, since a truck won't have the agility to avoid obstacles as well as a bike does and may not always be under full control.

West Mancos River Drainage

The West Mancos River cuts through resistant rocks west of Hesperus Mountain, producing striking vistas of canyons and basins high in the La Plata Mountains. Along the canyon of the West Mancos River there are several old roads, mining-camp and timber-mill sites, and trails that can take several full days to explore. Trails leading upstream also provide access to great views from the tops of several ridges, peaks, and passes. Though the canyon is a natural barrier, the West Mancos hiking trail links Sharkstooth Pass and Owen Basin at the upstream end, Transfer Campground and Box Canyon downstream.

It was in the upper West Mancos River drainage that gold was first discovered in the La Platas, possibly as early as the 1700s, by the Spanish priest, Father Salvero, and first mined by Captain George Jackson in 1892 on the river's north fork. Jackson set up placer operations below Slide Rock Basin, which later became known as Jackson City. He chased the placer gold up the river to its possible source and set up an underground mine with a water-powered stamp to crush the ore. A mining camp named Golconda was formed soon afterward, and it even had its own post office for several years.

The land north of the West Mancos canyon has been logged heavily over the years, predominantly between 1880 and 1910. Around 1900, a man named E. C. Cooper started the Spruce Mill about five miles northwest of Transfer Campground. The timber was cut in the surrounding area, processed into rough lumber, and hauled south to where it was stored and transferred to wagons headed for Mancos and the D&RG railroad. Hence the name Transfer. There were also lumber mills on Chicken and Turkey Creeks, and the remnants of one such mill can be seen on the Chicken Creek Trail. The road down from Spruce Mill to Transfer was steep, and there are many stories of wagons loaded with lumber losing their brakes and going out of control on the grades.

Transfer Campground

For camping and biking in the La Plata Mountains, Transfer Campground is the base camp location in the West Mancos drainage, and possibly the entire La Platas, with access to the largest number of rides. To get to Transfer, turn north off of U.S. Highway 160 at Mancos toward Dolores on Colorado 184. About 1/2 mile (1 kilometer) north of the intersection is a T with Montezuma County Road 42. Turn east toward Mancos State Recreation Area and Transfer Campground. Transfer is about 13 miles (21 kilometers) up this road.

The first hill that County Road 42 climbs out of the Mancos Valley is a terrace-outwash surface formed by glacial outwash carried by the ancestral Mancos River. It is capped by gravels and cobbles that are visible in road cuts. There are also problems with slope stability on this road because it is cut into the underlying Mancos Shale. Once riders are on top of the alluvial surface, they can see the La Platas rise up in the distance. The road travels over outwash all the way to Jackson Gulch Reservoir, and just past the turnoff there is a large quarry pit in the alluvium. About a mile (1-1/2 kilometers) past the turnoff the

At the closed road above Transfer Campground.

alluvium pinches out, and the road is on Dakota Sandstone that has had the overlying shale eroded away.

Transfer is a Forest Service campground with the usual amenities (drinking water and pit toilets). Seasonal use is designated by the Forest Service as June 1 through October 10. Several of the best rides out of Transfer are old roads that have been closed to motorized vehicles by slope failures and erosion but are still in good enough condition for mountain biking. The following profiles describe the most scenic and demanding of the many rides in the area that can be reached from Transfer Campground.

There are also a good number of cross-country ski trails accessible from Transfer, and there is nearly always plenty of snow from November to April. There are historical accounts describing workers hauling lumber on roads plowed through eight feet of snow at Transfer.

Jersey Jim Loop

Distance: 18.5 miles (30 kilometers) round trip

Difficulty: Rather long, good elevation gain; downhill on way out

Quadrangle: Rampart Hills, La Plata, Orphan Butte, Wallace Ranch

Time: 2 to 3 hours

Tips: Similar climb to that of Windy Gap

Elevation gain: 1,500 feet (460 meters)

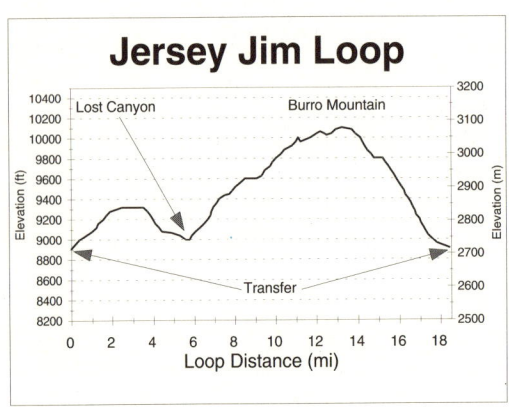

Description

This loop is a long ride with a good deal of elevation, but it is a good introduction to the La Plata Mountains. The route heads north out of Transfer (elevation 8,910 feet; 2,715 meters) on Forest Service Road (FS) 561 through aspen forests. In about 1 mile (1-1/2 kilometers) there is a junction with FS 561 taking off to the right and FS 560 to the left. Stay left and wind around, crossing Turkey Creek, Fish Creek, and Lost Canyon Creek. At about 7-1/2 miles (12

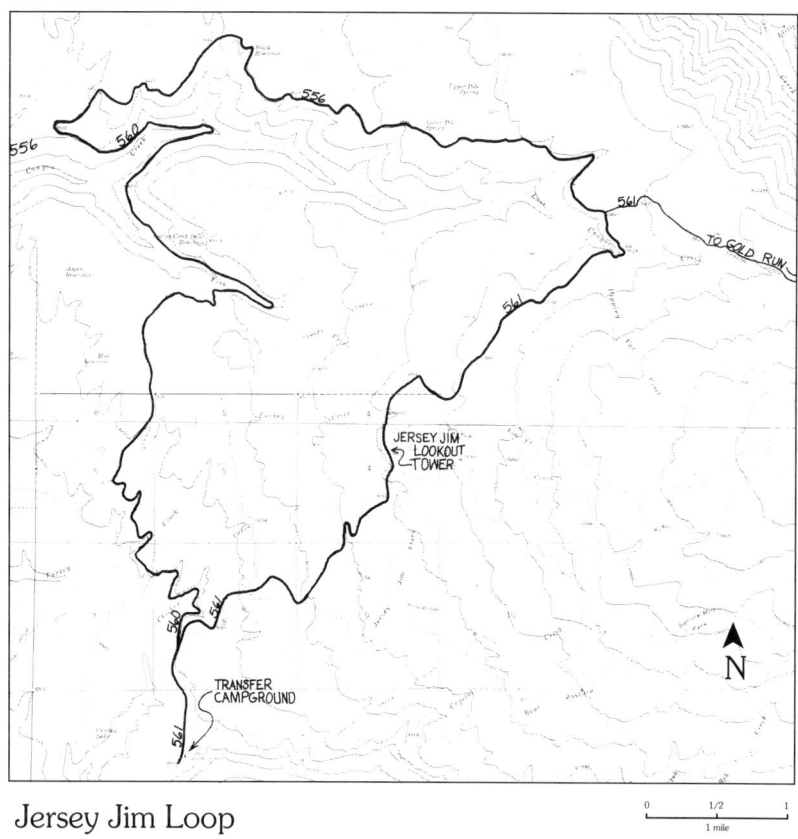

Jersey Jim Loop

kilometers) and the top of the north side of Lost Canyon, FS 560 ends at FS 556 (elevation 9,300 feet; 2,835 meters). Take a right here and climb on up to the east along the rim of Lost Canyon. After about 5-1/2 miles (9 kilometers) you reach the end of FS 556 at the junction with FS 561 (elevation 10,061 feet; 3,066 meters). A left turn here will take you on up to Gold Run Trail and Windy Gap, and a right will take you back down to Transfer via Jersey Jim. To Transfer is mostly downhill, but watch for cars and cows on the curves, some of which have limited visibility.

This ride stays for the most part in the aspen forest but gets into the subalpine fir and spruce forest in the higher elevations. Jersey Jim

The Jersey Jim Lookout Tower along the Jersey Jim Loop.

Lookout Tower was used for many years by the Forest Service to spot forest fires all across the western La Plata Mountains and Menefee and Mesa Verde. It is now out of commission except for use as a lodge of sorts, and it has a long waiting list of people who will pay to stay a night in the tower.

Geology

Most of the geology is obscured on this ride except for rock outcrops in Fish and Lost Creek Canyons. Transfer is situated on beds of upper Dakota Sandstone near the boundary with the Mancos Shale. As you drop into drainages, the fluvial sandstone of the Dakota is revealed and you drop farther in section across slopes of the Morrison Formation. After climbing up out of Lost Canyon there is little to see because you are riding in the lower Mancos Shale that has been uplifted and covers an igneous core that outcrops at Burro Mountain to the north.

Morrison Trail 610

Distance: 10 miles (16 kilometers)
Difficulty: Moderate to technical
Quadrangle: Rampart Hills, Wallace Ranch
Time: 4 to 6 hours
Tips: Not terribly long, but can be exhausting with a big uphill on return trip.
Elevation gain: 1,200 feet (366 meters)

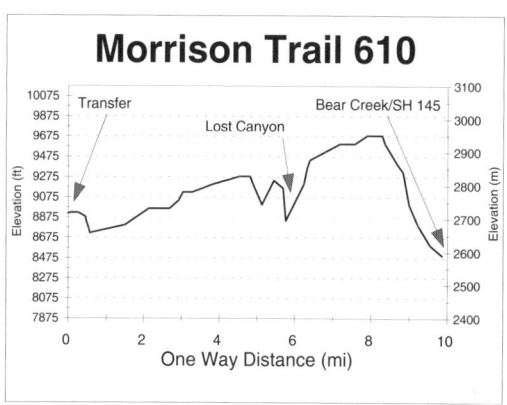

Description

One of the best marked and maintained trails in the Transfer Campground area is the Morrison Trail. It runs from the bottom of Chicken Creek Canyon from the Chicken Creek Trail north across several roads and through canyons to the edge of Bear Creek Canyon. From there it drops on into Bear Creek, coming out at the Bear Creek trailhead on Colorado 45 and the Dolores River. Many stretches of the trail are tough to ride because of the grade or technical conditions, but it is a ride that feels very isolated from the rest of the area.

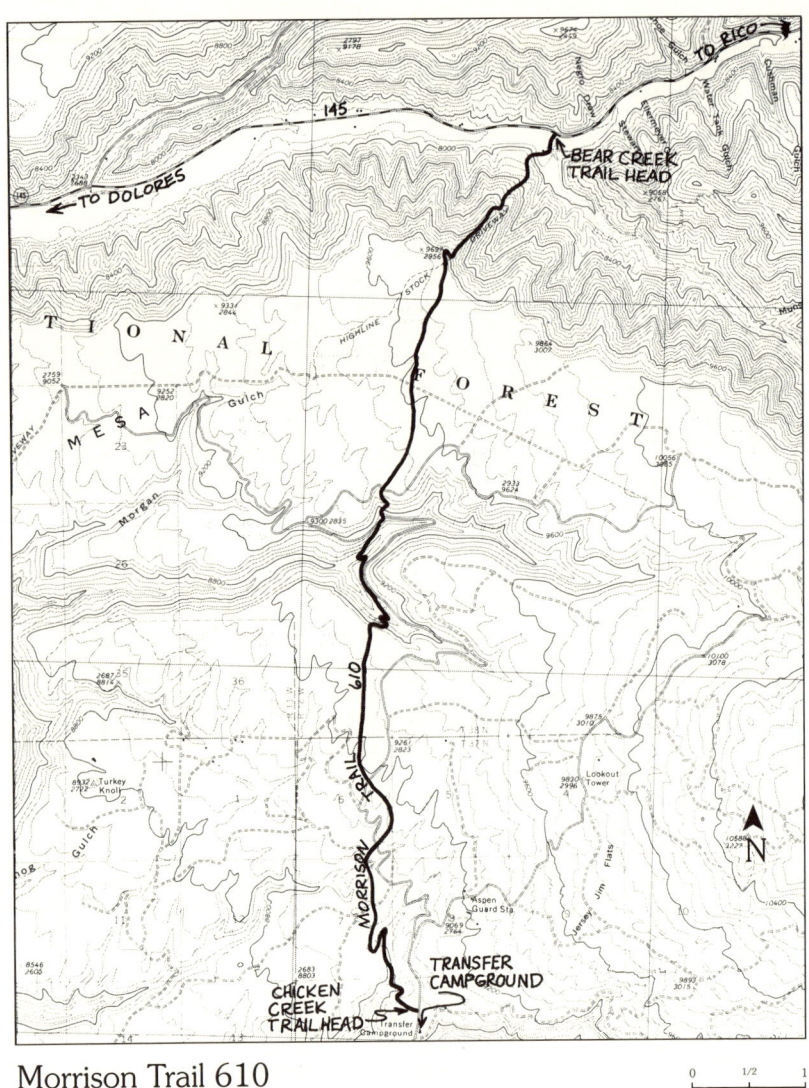

Morrison Trail 610

To reach the trailhead, take the Chicken Creek Trail from just north of Transfer Campground, west off of FS 560, and drop into Chicken Creek Canyon. The trail winds to the bottom, where the head of the Morrison Trail is well marked with a sign. Turn right, and

Riding through aspen on Morrison Trail 610; the area on the right has been logged.

head up the canyon. Again, the trail is well marked as it crosses roads, and there are narrow bridges across irrigation ditches. After crossing Fish Creek and Lost Canyon Creek, the trail climbs steeply over a narrow rocky trail toward FS 560. It is a good idea to turn left on 560 and climb to FS 556, take a right, and ride for about half a mile (1 kilometer) to the trail. The trail is rather difficult between these two roads. From here it is only about 4-1/2 miles (7 kilometers) to the Bear Creek trailhead, though there is a lot of elevation drop into the canyon that must be made up on the way back.

There are several roads crossing on this trail, so at different places you can get on FS 560 to get back to Transfer easier. The trail can also be a point-to-point ride if you arrange a pickup at Colorado 45.

The trail down into Bear Creek can be difficult and is not as well maintained as are other trails in the area.

Geology

The trail drops off the Mancos Shale and Dakota Sandstone to cross the Morrison Formation as it crosses the Chicken Creek, Fish Creek, and Lost Canyon Creek Canyons and drops farther down-section across the Dolores Formation and Entrada Sandstone. In Bear Creek Canyon there are views of the Cutler Formation red beds farther up the canyon.

Golconda

Distance: 7 miles (11.3 kilometers) round trip
Difficulty: Extremely difficult
Quadrangle: Rampart Hills
Time: 2 to 4 hours round trip
Tips: This trail is recommended only for advanced riders looking for very technical stretches
Elevation gain: 750 feet (230 meters)

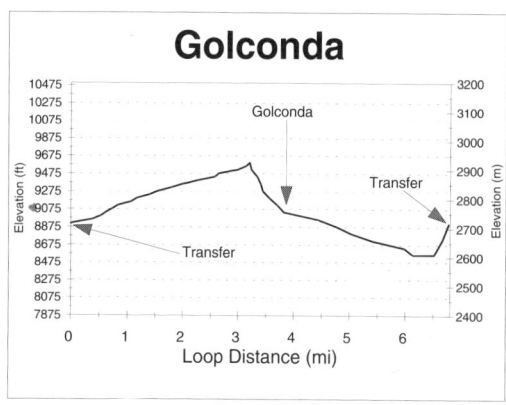

Description

Golconda is the location of an old mining camp that was in operation around the turn of the century. Nothing is left now from those days except the feeling of what it might have been like to have lived in the bottom of the upper West Mancos Canyon, where in the winter there can be more than five feet of snow at any given time. Some small-scale surface placer mining continued through the mid-1980s, though the Forest Service has been working to restore the river bottom for wildlife habitat. Perhaps someday the bottom of the canyon will again look as it did when the first prospectors dipped their pans into the river.

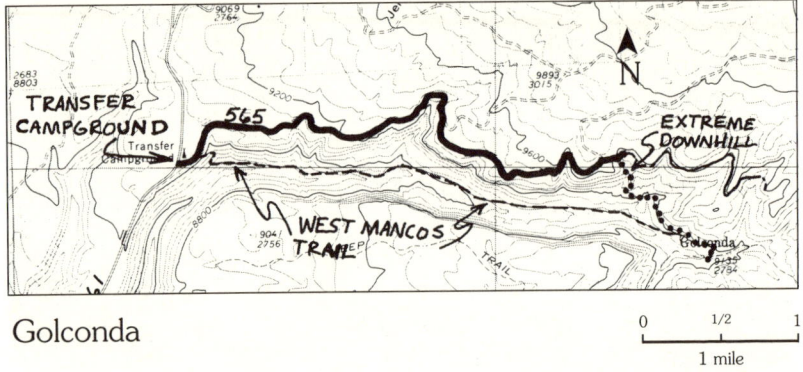

Golconda

The route to Golconda begins at the West Mancos overlook (elevation 8,910 feet; 2,716 meters) near Transfer Campground and heads up the old closed road that follows the edge of the canyon (FS 565). The road is closed to automobiles at 1-3/4 miles (2.8 kilometers), just before several landslides heavily damage it. At the same place, outcrops of the upper Mancos Shale are exposed in the road-cut. At approximately 2 miles (3.2 kilometers), the road crosses Crystal Creek and branches (elevation 9,369 feet; 2,856 meters). Stay right on FS 565—the other branch heads through Beef Pasture on its way to Windy Gap. In another mile (1-1/2 kilometer) the road bends sharply back to the west, and another fork is reached (elevation 9,640 feet; 2,938 meters). Again take a right, this time onto FS 348, and after another short distance, notice a sign indicating that the insanely steep path to the right is closed to motorized vehicles. Turn right and drop down into the canyon toward Golconda. The road drops 505 feet (154 meters) in a little over half a mile (1 kilometer) to the West Mancos Trail. Be careful of the rocks in the path and the erosional channels. This part of the trail may be ridden by the more courageous, but be careful because it is a fair piece over rough terrain to get help. At the West Mancos Trail, turn left to go to Golconda, which is about 3 miles (2 kilometers) away over much better trail.

At Golconda there is a nice place to relax and eat some food while looking over the river bottom, now somewhat remediated after years of placer mining. The river is difficult to cross until August or later except in the driest years. From here you can climb up to the Owen Basin Trail, which will also take you to the Sharkstooth Trail. This route is very steep and rough, so you might want to get to this area from the

Dropping down into Golconda.

top on the rides to follow. The trail back to where you reached the West Mancos Trail is deceivingly nice compared to what is in store over the 4-1/2 miles (7 kilometers) back to Transfer.

The West Mancos and Transfer Trails that lead back to Transfer are about 50 percent rideable, 30 percent technical to unrideable, and there are some good climbs near the end when you are working your way out of the canyon. There are nice views of the canyon and the cliffs of intrusive igneous rocks along the way.

Geology

Transfer Campground is situated on a caprock of Dakota Sandstone, though the picturesque cliffs along the West Mancos Canyon are composed of igneous intrusive rocks that forced their way out from the igneous core of the La Plata Mountains along the weak boundary between the Dakota Sandstone and the Mancos Shale. Just east of the campground you will climb onto the Mancos Shale, which will be apparent in the slumping of the road down the slope. The road is located just above the contact between the igneous intrusion and the Mancos Shale, and in some road-cuts the shale is harder than normal where it was baked by the heat of the intruding magma below. Dropping down to Golconda, you once again cross the Dakota Sandstone and a small slice of the Morrison Formation before reaching the fluvial deposits that fill in the bottom of the valley. The road leaving Transfer can be a good example of the problems associated with the Mancos Shale if a thunderstorm saturates the road.

The fluvial deposits were transported by the West Mancos River from the igneous core of the La Plata Mountains, and the process eroded and sorted the heavier minerals such as gold and pyrite, which have been extracted from the rest of the sediment by hydraulic sluice operations. The source of gold in the Golconda area is in hydrothermal veins along the edge of the igneous intrusive core. This contact can be seen upstream from Golconda where the north and south forks of the river cut through resistant reddish brown–stained igneous rocks.

# North Fork

Distance: 12 miles (19.5 kilometers) round trip
Difficulty: Moderate to technical
Quadrangle: Rampart Hills, La Plata
Time: 2 to 3 hours
Tips: Watch for sharp rocks near river crossing. Good hiking trails at North Fork
Elevation gain: 1,250 feet (381 meters)

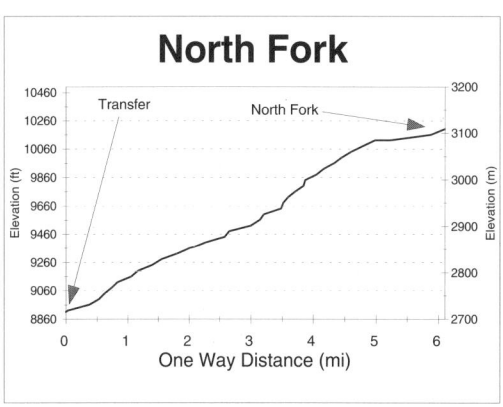

Description

North Fork is a local name for the area where an old mining and logging road once crossed the North Fork of the West Mancos River. Upstream from the river crossing, where the river cuts through some iron-stained intrusive rocks, are the remnants of the mining camp named Jackson City. Captain Jackson was the first prospector to find gold in the area, and in the ruins of Jackson City there are parts of an old ore stamp that was brought in to process hard-rock ore.

This route avoids the more heavily traveled and maintained roads, following the same initial trail that the Golconda ride used on FS 565,

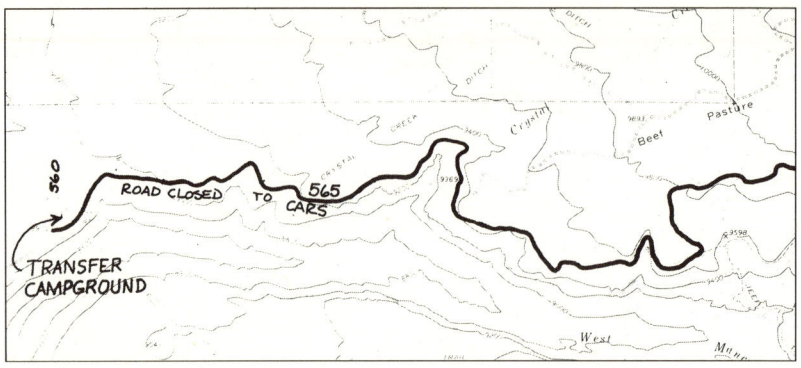

North Fork

but instead of dropping off into the canyon, stay on the old road, climbing up and across the side of the mountain. After about two more miles there is a fork in the road (elevation 10,200 feet; 3,108 meters), and the right fork (FS 347) leads to North Fork. From the branch, the old road traverses the slope and drops for another two miles to an old mining and timber camp on the North Fork of the West Mancos River (elevation 10,110 feet; 3,082 meters). The site is still used occasionally by hunters and campers. The trail continues across the river for about one mile. Forests south of the river were logged heavily, and there are many old logging roads crisscrossing the slopes.

North Fork is a popular place to begin ascents of Hesperus Mountain via the west ridge. The hike to the top of Hesperus Mountain takes about six hours and is for the most part nontechnical. There is good elk habitat in the timber south of the river and a good campsite west of the river crossing. In the late summer and early fall, bull elk can be heard bugling in the timber.

The trail between the Golconda route and the river crossing can be treacherous during thunderstorms because of the amount of mud that is produced by rain.

Geology

The road north along the West Mancos River canyon follows a sill intrusion at the contact between the lower Mancos Shale and the

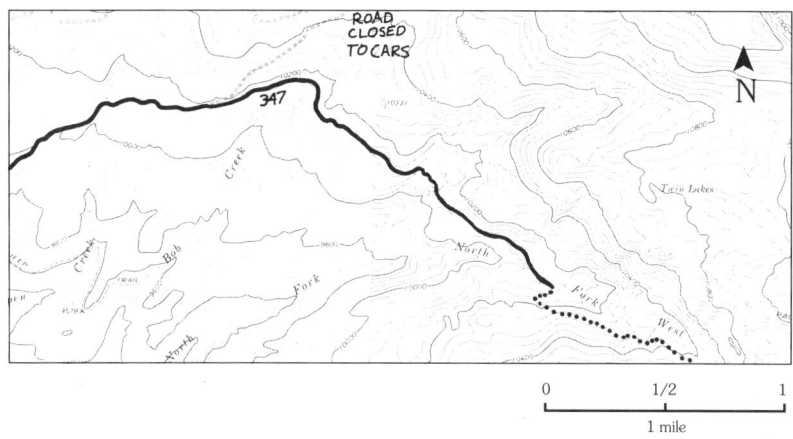

upper Dakota Sandstone. The trail climbs onto the Mancos Shale and stays on it all the way to the North Fork crossing. At the crossing, more sill intrusions can be seen on the side of Hesperus Mountain, where they form light gray cliffs.

Crossing the North Fork of the West Mancos River.

Notice the change in the Mancos Shale as you approach the river crossing. It becomes much harder and breaks into slatey and prismatic pieces. This is due to the contact metamorphism from the heat of the igneous intrusions. The harder rock fragments can puncture tires on occasion. Across the river to the south is a large field of slide rock with ridges and swales produced by landslide-type flows. This is referred to as a rock glacier–type flow of talus that was produced over the last fifteen to twenty thousand years, since the last ice age. Boulders and cobbles in the slide are angular with sharp edges but can be crossed on foot. Most of the talus has resulted from rocks toppling from cliffs of diorite and metamorphosed shale on the ridge extending west from Hesperus Mountain. Large masses of slide rock or talus are common around the bases of peaks of all mountains in southwest Colorado and were produced by thousands of years of freezing and thawing and changing climates.

 Windy Gap/Twin Lakes

Distance: 19 miles (30.5 kilometers) round trip
Difficulty: Long; elevation gain; easy return trip
Quadrangle: Rampart Hills, La Plata
Time: 2 to 4 hours round trip
Tips: Serious climb at elevation; great views from Windy Gap area and several historic sites
Elevation gain: 2,200 feet (670 meters)

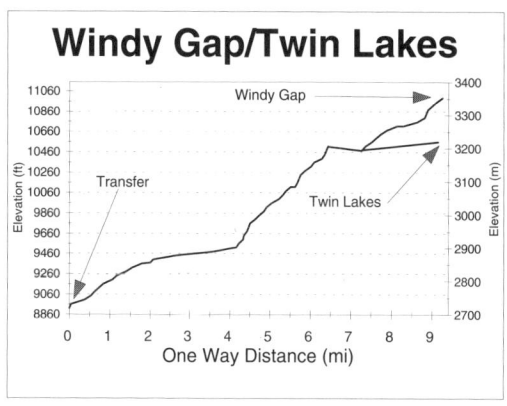

Description

Take the same initial road (FS 565) that leads to both Golconda and North Fork, but turn left on an old road that leads up the slope just past Crystal Creek to FS 350. This road climbs, climbs, and climbs through Beef Pasture (elevation 9,893 feet; 3,015 meters) and Spruce Mill Park (elevation 10,520 feet; 3,206 meters) in three miles. The road then traverses the slope and actually drops a bit until at about 4 miles (6-1/2 kilometers) there is a T in the road; continue on FS 350 and climb for 2 miles (3 kilometers) to a fork in the road (elevation 10,720 feet; 3,268 meters). Take a right on FS 348 to go to

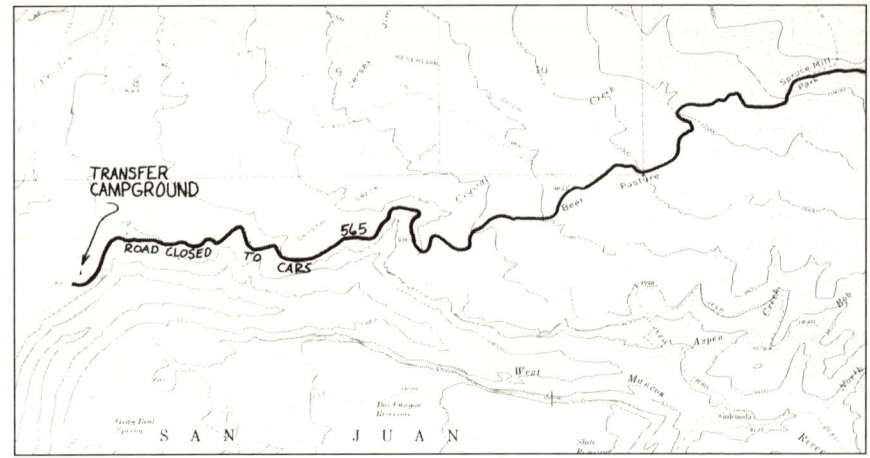

Windy Gap/Twin Lakes

Twin Lakes; a left, remaining on FS 350, leads to Windy Gap. Windy Gap (elevation 11,000 feet; 3,353 meters) is about 1 mile (1.5 kilometers) and Twin Lakes (elevation 10,800 feet; 3,292 meters) is about half a mile (1 kilometer). About 1-1/4 miles (2 kilometers) past Twin Lakes is the trailhead for Sharkstooth Pass (elevation 11,160 feet; 3,402 meters), some of which is rideable but is generally tough because it is very steep and climbs to 11,936 feet (3,638 meters). The view from the top is spectacular and enthusiastically recommended, even if it means hiking from this point, which is advisable in most circumstances.

There are several other roads that loop back around and down to Transfer Campground, including FS 561, which winds around the north side of Burro Mountain with great views of Bear Creek Canyon and beyond.

As you ride through Spruce Mill Park, up the slope to the left is the location of Spruce Mill, which was in operation around 1900. The mill was owned by E. C. Cooper, who moved it to this location when his sons Sam and Jack were young boys. If you look up the slope, you can imagine a day when the loggers were rolling logs down the slope from wagons to the mill. On one day in particular, E. C. looked out to see his son Jack walking out across the slope, unaware that a log had

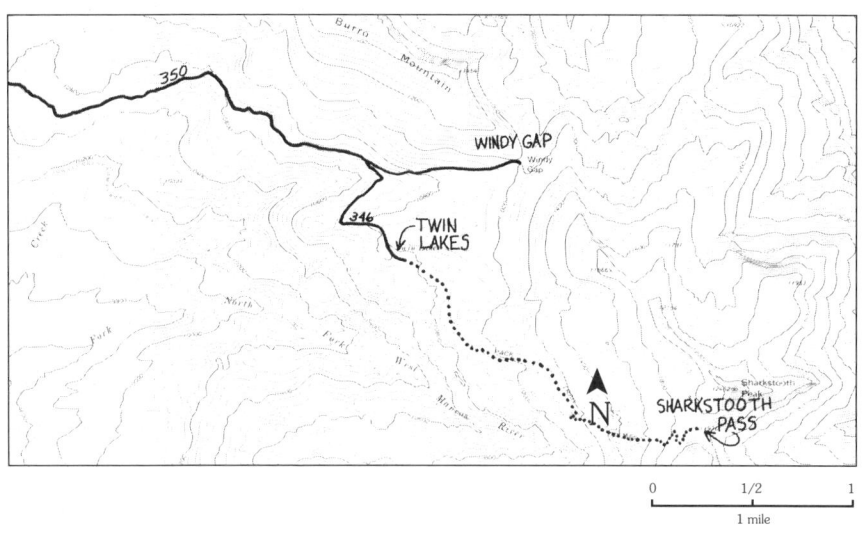

Cruising through Spruce Mill Park on the way to Windy Gap and Twin Lakes.

just been released and was picking up steam, heading right for him. Luckily for Jack, however, he stumbled and fell headlong into a small depression, and the log bounced over him.

Geology

The road north (FS 565) along the West Mancos River canyon follows a sill intrusion at the contact between the lower Mancos Shale and the upper Dakota Sandstone. The trail climbs onto the Mancos Shale and stays on it all the way to the North Fork crossing. At the crossing, more sill intrusions can be seen on the side of Hesperus Mountain, where they form light gray cliffs.

Notice the change in the Mancos Shale as you approach the river crossing. It becomes much harder and breaks into slatey and prismatic pieces. This is due to the contact metamorphism from the heat of the igneous intrusions. The harder rock fragments can puncture tires on occasion. Across the river to the south is a large field of slide rock with ridges and swales produced by flow. This is referred to as a rock glacier, as described on pages 39 and 74. Boulders and cobbles in the slide are angular with sharp edges but can be crossed on foot. Most of the talus has resulted from rocks toppling from cliffs of diorite and metamorphosed shale on the ridge extending west from Hesperus Mountain. Large masses of slide rock or talus are common around the bases of peaks of all mountains in southwest Colorado.

Chicken Creek Trail

Distance: 14 miles (22.5 kilometers)
Difficulty: Hard; technical, with unrideable stretches
Quadrangle: Rampart Hills, Millwood
Time: 2 to 4 hours
Tips: Can be frustratingly unrideable in spots
Elevation gain: 1,200 feet (366 meters)

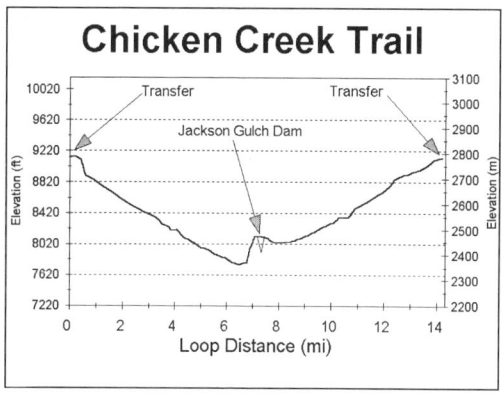

Description

This trail drops off westward into Chicken Creek Canyon just north of Transfer Campground, switchbacking down the slope. These switchbacks are for the most part rideable, though there is at least one place where a tree has fallen across the trail. At the bottom of the canyon is a sign indicating that it is eight miles to Jackson Lake. Take a left and follow the trail, crossing back and forth across the creek, which can be dry for most of the late summer and fall, especially in dry years. The trail is sometimes used for moving cattle and is not very well maintained—roots and logs impede progress—but on the

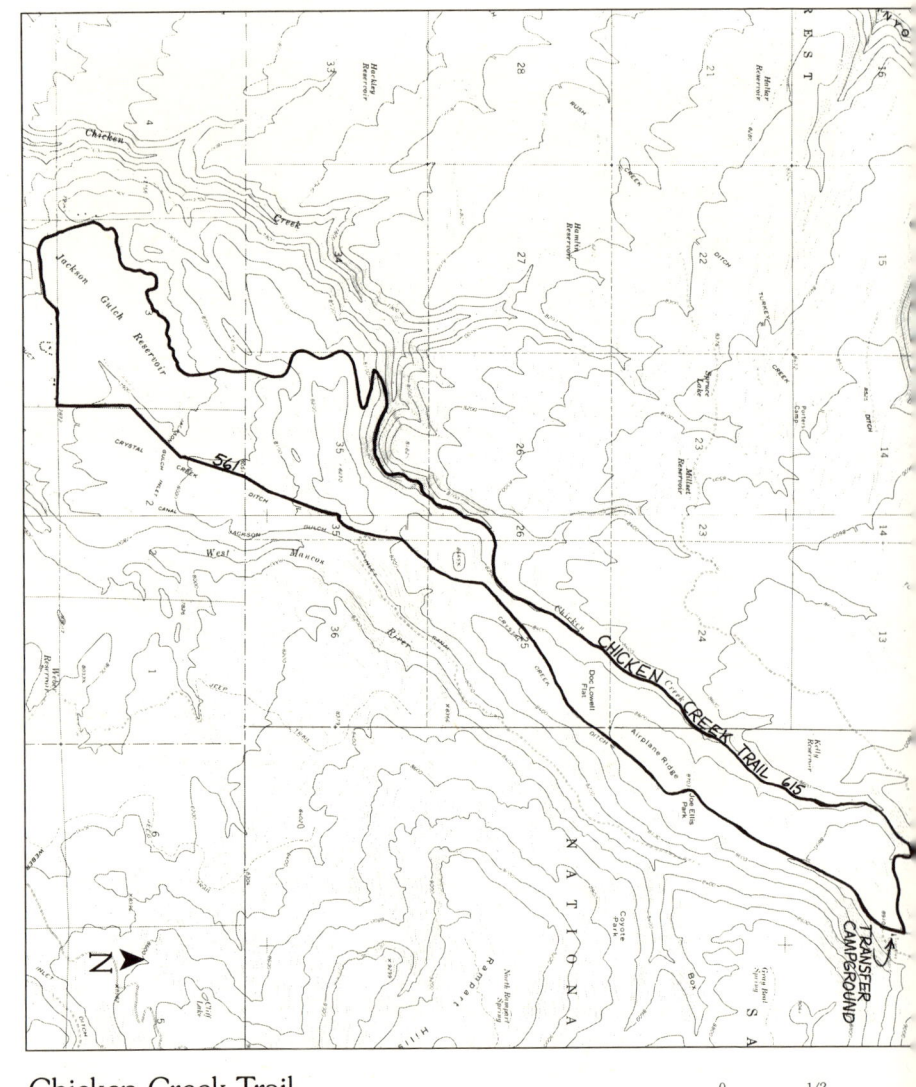

Chicken Creek Trail

At Transfer Campground, near the Chicken Creek Trailhead.

other hand, it is a good place to work on technical riding skills. After about six miles, the trail finally climbs up out of the canyon and tops out on Jackson Gulch Dam and the Mancos State Recreation Area. Here you can get more water (by this point my two bottles are usually dry) and return to Transfer via County Road 42.

Geology

The trail drops off of the Dakota Sandstone caprock and zigzags down slopes formed on Morrison Formation. This trail can, like many others, get mucky during rainstorms because of the clay in the upper Morrison. At the bottom of the canyon the trail winds across the channel of Chicken Creek, which is mantled by boulders and cobbles of Dakota Sandstone, armoring the channel that would normally cut easily through the Morrison. The climb up to Jackson Gulch Reservoir is also rocky from the Dakota Sandstone. From the reservoir back to Transfer you are riding up the dip of the sandstone beds at the contact point with thousands of feet of Mancos Shale that has been removed.

Gold Run Loop

Distance: 18 miles (29 kilometers) round trip
Difficulty: Hard; some technical creek crossings; downhill on way out
Quadrangle: Rampart Hills, Orphan Butte, Wallace Ranch
Time: 3 to 4 hours
Tips: Climb similar to Windy Gap
Elevation gain: 2,267 feet (691 meters)

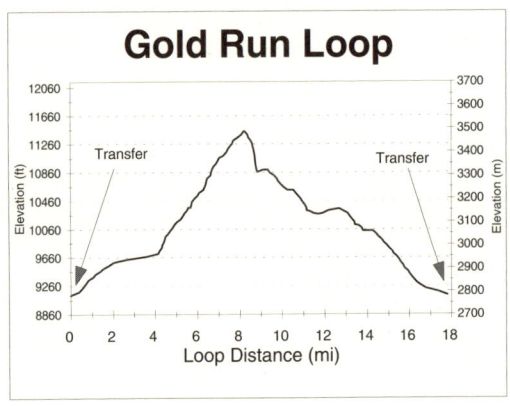

Description

Take the same initial road (FS 565 to 350) that leads to Windy Gap/Twin Lakes, and turn left on an old road that leads up the slope just past Crystal Creek (2.2 miles; 3.5 kilometers) to FS 350, and then take a left at Spruce Mill Park (5-1/2 miles; 9 kilometers). At 6.2 miles (10 kilometers) this old road reaches FS 351 at a place where the Forest Service has plowed up earth to close the road to automobiles (elevation 10,826 feet; 3,300 meters). Take a right here and

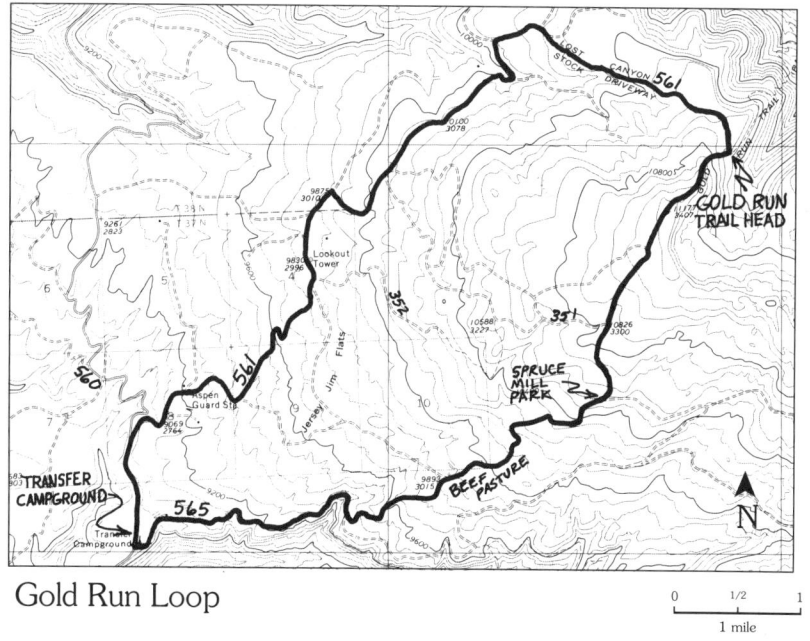

Gold Run Loop

head on up toward the Gold Run trailhead and FS 561, which is over the hill (elevation 11,177 feet; 3,407 meters) and about 1-1/2 miles (2-1/2 kilometers) away. At the Gold Run trailhead, turn left and west, dropping down toward the Jersey Jim Lookout Tower and Transfer.

 Chicken Creek Road Loop

Distance: 13.5 miles (21 kilometers) round trip
Difficulty: Not technical, but significant elevation change
Quadrangle: Rampart Hills, Millwood
Time: 3 to 4 hours
Tips: Long, gradual ride through foothills ponderosa environment
Elevation gain: 610 feet (186 meters)

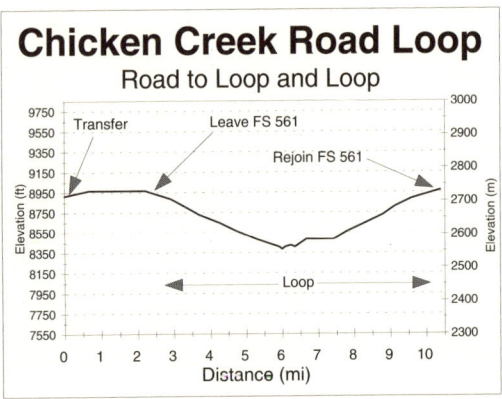

Description

Ride north from Transfer Campground on FS 560 for about 1 mile (1.5 kilometers) to a junction with FS 561 that takes off to the right to Jersey Jim. Bear left, staying on 560. After crossing both forks of Chicken Creek, there will be a turnoff to the left (FS 385). Take it and drop down onto the interfluve between Chicken and Turkey Creeks. After about half a mile (1 kilometer) there will be a fork in the road (elevation 8,960 feet; 2,731 meters) where FS 385 takes off to the left; FS 559 is to the right. Take a left and ride downhill through

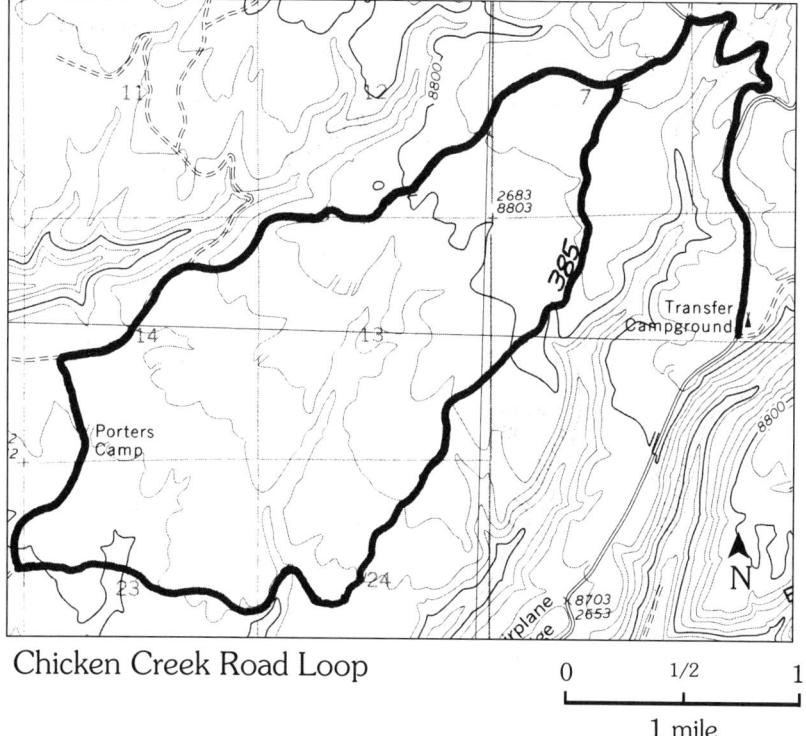

Chicken Creek Road Loop

the ponderosa pines for about 4.5 miles (7.5 kilometers) to another junction (elevation 8,376 feet; 2,553 meters) just past Spruce Lake. Take a right on the unmarked road and climb past Porters Camp to another junction (elevation 8,525 feet; 2,600 meters) where you take another right on FS 559. Climb for about 3.5 miles (5.5 kilometers) back to FS 385, return to FS 560, and head south to Transfer Campground.

The landscape along this ride is not as dramatic as on others, but the forest can be very serene and beautiful when there has been a wet spring or when the aspen and oak brush are changing colors in mid-September. There is also a healthy population of deer and elk in this area.

Geology

This trail remains almost entirely on top of the Dakota Sandstone, though there is a variable amount of the remnants of the Mancos Shale.

Transfer to Millwood

Distance: 24 miles (39 kilometers) round trip
Difficulty: Moderate
Quadrangle: Rampart Hills, Millwood
Time: 4 to 5 hours
Tips: Similar to the Haycamp Point ride, but is on the other side of Lost Canyon and ends up near Joe Moore Reservoir
Elevation gain: 1,400 feet (427 meters)

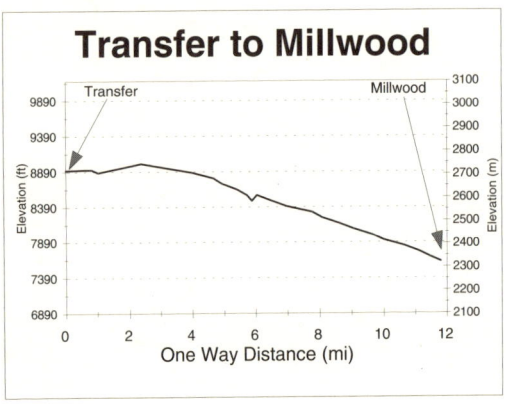

Description

Take the Chicken Creek Road route north from Transfer Campground on FS 560, but skip the Chicken Creek turnoff and proceed to FS 559, also known as the Millwood Road, at the sign about 2.5 miles (4 kilometers) north of Transfer. Follow 559 all the way, dropping gradually down to Millwood. From this point, Joe Moore Reservoir is about a mile to the east, and several other roads and trails lead down Lost Canyon and through the woods around Joe Moore. There are several short rides out of Millwood as well, and they are

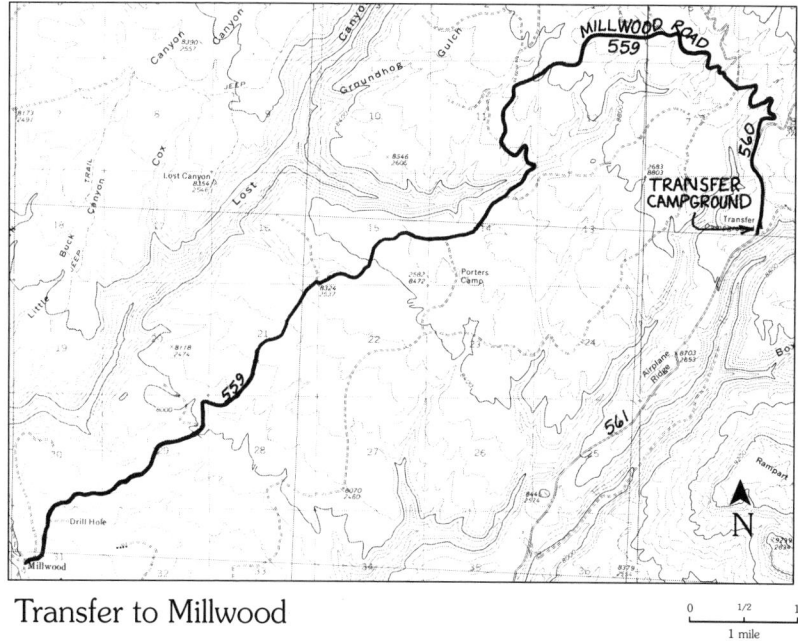

Transfer to Millwood

described briefly on page 76. Millwood itself is an old railroad loading point for pine timber cut from the forest to the north and east. The restaurant in Mancos called Millwood Junction is named after that station. In the late 1800s, the rail extended through Millwood and down lower Lost Canyon.

There is some private land that is crossed by FS 559 and quite a bit of stock in the area, so be careful, because there is some vehicle traffic and cows wandering about.

Geology

The geology along this ride is virtually identical to that described for Haycamp Point: the trail travels over a thin layer of residual Mancos Shale over the Dakota Sandstone, and canyons cut into the Morrison Formation.

# Haycamp Point

Distance: 42 miles (68 kilometers) round trip
Difficulty: Hard
Quadrangle: Rampart Hills, Wallace Ranch, Stoner
Time: 3 to 4 hours
Tips: This is a long ride and no water can be counted on, so take plenty
Elevation gain: 1,220 feet (372 meters maximum relief)

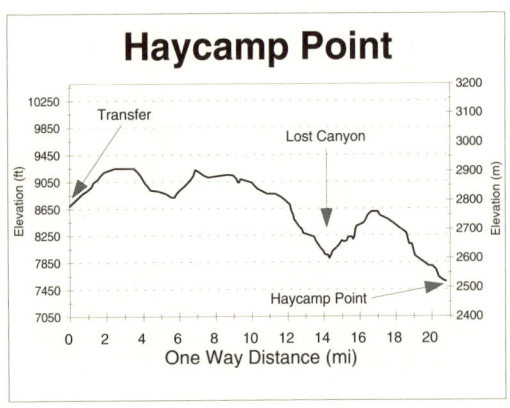

Description

Haycamp Point is an overlook into the beautiful Dolores River canyon at the mouth of Spruce Water Canyon. The road/trail crosses Lost Canyon and winds on to the west toward the north-south-trending Dolores River. Starting at Transfer Campground, head north on FS 561 for 1 mile (1.5 kilometers) to a junction marked with signs indicating that taking a right will follow FS 561 to Jersey Jim and a left will follow 560 to Haycamp Mesa. Follow FS 560 on around

Views from the Lost Canyon Overlook, a side trip off of Haycamp Point.

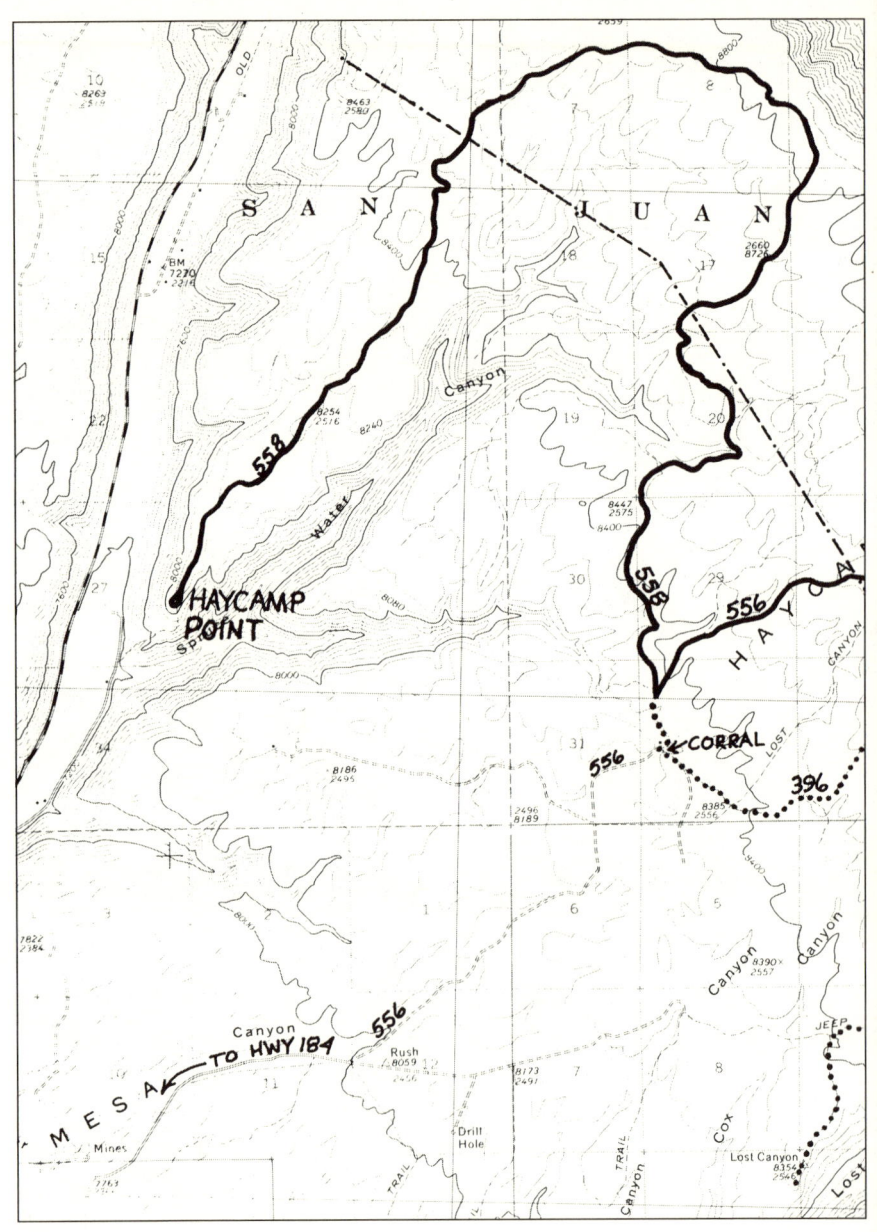

Haycamp Point

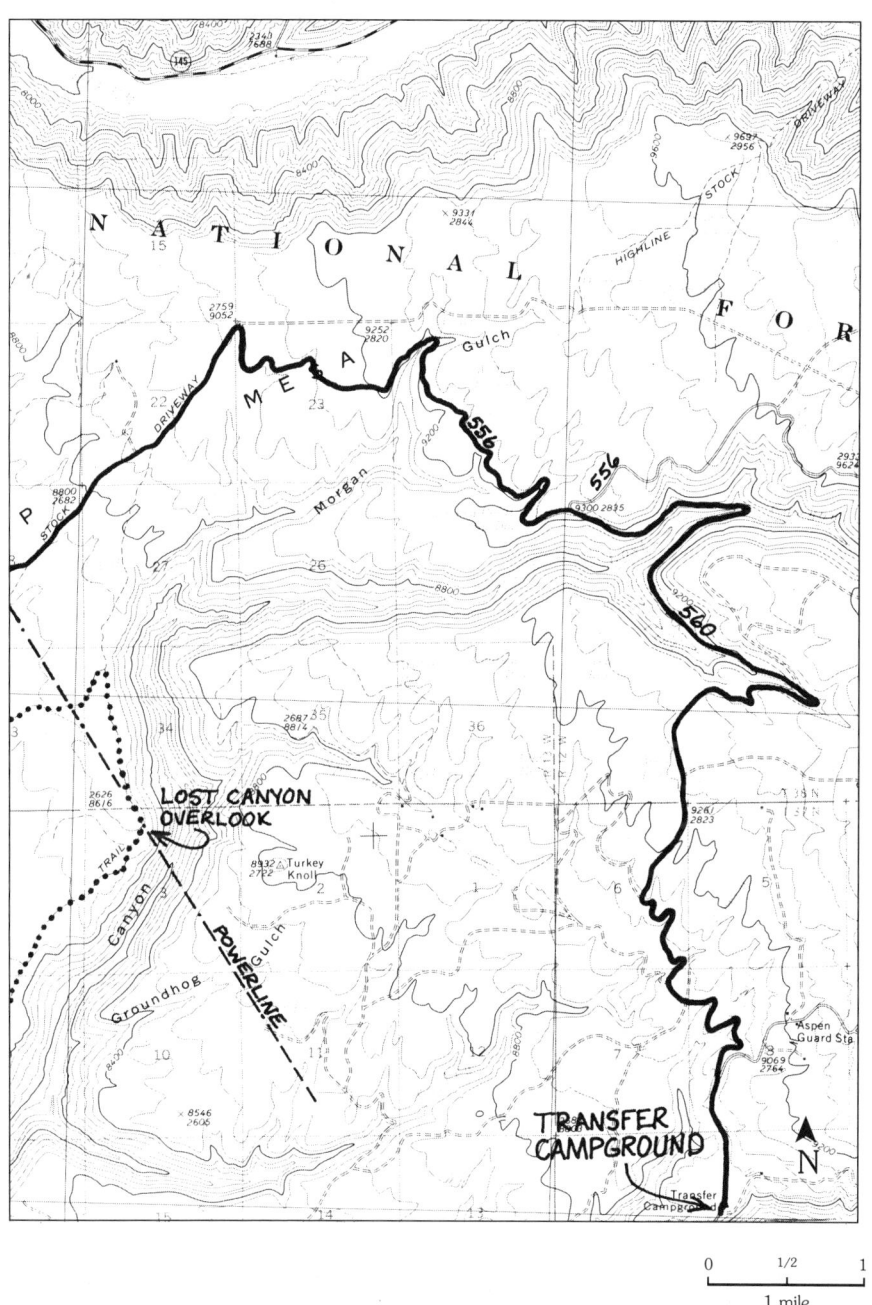

through Lost Canyon to FS 556 as described for the Jersey Jim Loop, but turn left on FS 556 and wind around the rim of Lost Canyon for about 3 miles (5 kilometers), until you drop onto Haycamp Mesa. About 2 miles (3.5 kilometers) later, you will reach the junction of FS 556 and 558. Another kilometer and you cross a small creekbed and reach FS 396 to the Lost Canyon Overlook. The road is improved but rough all the way to this point.

This trail can also be reached from SH 184 about 18 miles (29 kilometers) north of Mancos. At the sign indicating Forest Service access road Haycamp Mesa, turn east and drive for about 15 miles (24 kilometers) on FS 556 to the branch with FS 558, just past a large corral that is near the turnoff to Lost Canyon on FS 396. From this side the trail is about 25 miles (40 kilometers) to Haycamp Point and back, and 7.5 miles (12 kilometers) to the Lost Canyon overlook and back.

At this point, FS 558 is still well taken care of, but as you wind around the north end of Spruce Water Canyon it gets progressively more primitive until it is little more than a trail when it stops at Haycamp Point. There are some muddy spots and ruts, but the sandy roadbed dries very quickly after rains. It is a long climb back to the junction with 556. At Haycamp Point there is a good view of the Dolores River valley and Spruce Water Canyon through the large old ponderosas. On the road north of Haycamp Point there are tracts of logged and replanted pines from the late sixties or early seventies.

The road to Lost Canyon overlook is unimproved and can be rutted with frequent water-filled depressions. This road winds around to the north and climbs before reaching an old logging road that follows the edge of Lost Canyon. You start to realize that the canyon is close, though the stands of aspen and pine conceal the view for the most part. Heading right and along the rim, notice a power line that you crossed under before reaching this road. This power line will get progressively closer, and as you drop down off of the first real descent, it will be directly above. Pick a trail to the left, and ride underneath the lines to the canyon's edge. There are cliffs along the road composed of Dakota Sandstone that afford a great view of the canyon and Hesperus Mountain.

Geology

This trail follows the top of the Dakota Sandstone for the most part, dropping into canyons and the Morrison Formation periodically.

South-facing slopes covered by aspens and oak brush can exhibit soil-creep, indicated by trees bent at their trunks as the base is rotated, with their tops remaining vertical. Lobes of soil bulging under the carpet of grass are also signs of soil deformation.

On FS 558 from Akin Reservoir to Haycamp Point there are alluvial gravels and cobbles that were probably transported by the Dolores River before it cut through the Dakota Sandstone and became entrenched in its modern valley.

T-Down Corral

T-Down Corral is located in scenic T-Down Park and provides access to some of the most photogenic subalpine country in the La Platas. Take County Road 44 north from U.S. 160 approximately 3 miles (5 kilometers) east of Mancos (look for the Echo Basin and Echo Basin Dude Ranch signs). This road turns to gravel and becomes FS 566, winding up the hills through oak brush for about 6 miles (10 kilometers) to a junction. The junction is in a saddle with the Hogback to the east and T-Down Park to the west. Take a left on FS 331 and drive down to the corral.

This area is open to camping, though during hunting season (October and November) it is a bit crowded, and biking in the area then is not advised because of the weather. There is no campground, and although there are many good camping spots on Rampart Hills and higher on Burnt Ridge and Echo Basin, care should be taken to leave the area in the same condition as it was found. This area is still in the San Juan National Forest, and any questions or comments should be taken to the Mancos Ranger District office.

T-Down Park sits on top of a sill-like igneous intrusion that has created the Rampart Hills. Below the Rampart Hills is an apron that can be ridden on to traverse the cliffs and reach some very serene meadows and vistas. The area below the Rampart Hills is covered by oak brush, but there is a four-wheel-drive road that wraps around the base. The tops of the hills are covered by ponderosa and oak-brush forest.

Rampart Hills

Distance: 2.5 miles (4 kilometers) round trip
Difficulty: Short and easy
Quadrangle: Rampart Hills
Time: 1 hour
Tips: Nice evening or morning warm-up ride or picnic spot with a great view
Elevation gain: 400 feet (122 meters)

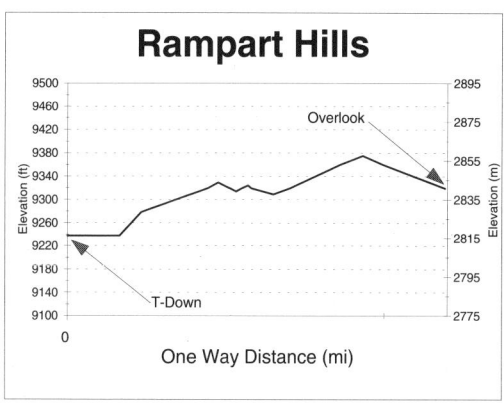

Description

This is a short ride out to the edge of the old intrusion that is weathered to form jagged cliffs. The precipice forms an overlook where the Mancos and Montezuma Valleys and Mesa Verde, Ute Mountain, and the Abajo Mountains of southeastern Utah can be seen. Take the small road from T-Down to the west out onto the natural rampart over a small elevation gain, then drop to the edge in about 1.5 miles (2.5 kilometers). Sunsets can be spectacular from this spot.

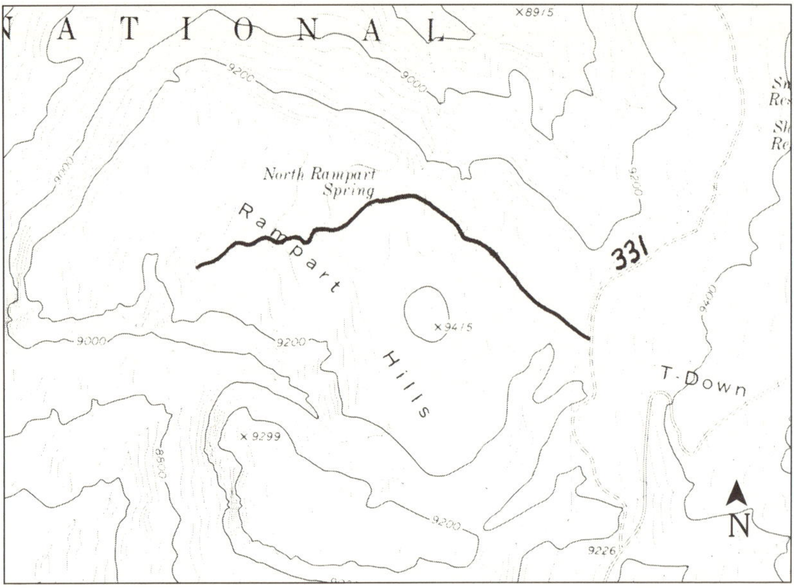

Rampart Hills

0 1/2 1
1 mile

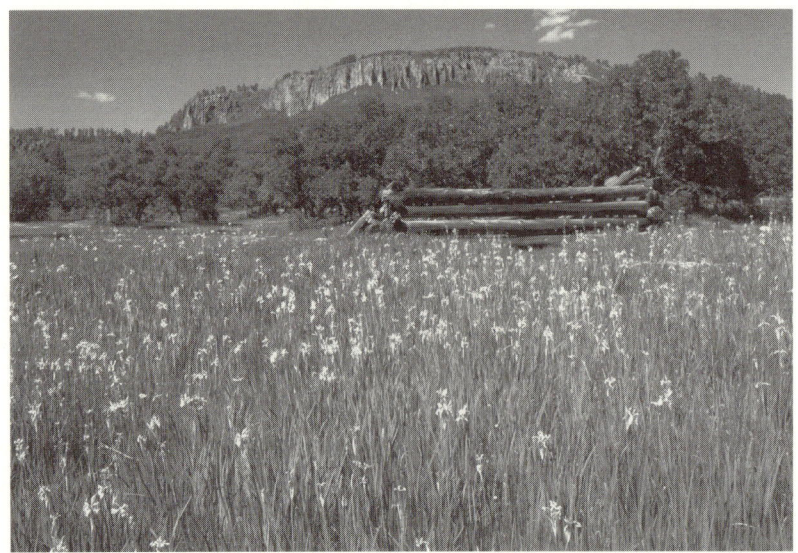

Iris patch and cabin in front of Rampart Hills.

Geology

The view from the Rampart Hills is looking out off a large igneous intrusion capped by a thin layer of Mancos Shale. The Mancos Shale also formed the slopes below when the intruding magma pushed between beds of the shale. In the distance is the cuesta of Mesa Verde and the Point Lookout Sandstone of the Mesa Verde Group supporting Point Lookout. On the western horizon are the Abajo (also known as the Blue) Mountains, which are located just west of Monticello, Utah. These mountains, and Sleeping Ute Mountain, to the left, are formed by laccolithic intrusions similar to the La Plata Mountains.

# Graybeal Spring

Distance: 9.5 miles (15 kilometers)
Difficulty: Moderate
Quadrangle: Rampart Hills
Time: 1 to 2 hours
Tips: Nice view of West Mancos
Elevation gain: 560 feet (171 meters) round trip

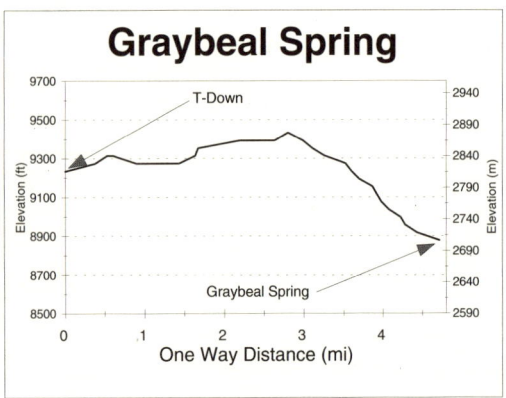

Description

Take FS 331 north out of T-Down Park for four miles around the east end of Box Canyon to where it becomes a trail. Here it turns west and drops for about three miles to Graybeal Spring. Out on the edge of the point there is a pretty good view of West Mancos Canyon.

Graybeal Spring is named after one of the first cowboys to build a cabin in the Mancos Valley—Wylie Graybeal, who started a ranch down in the valley around 1880.

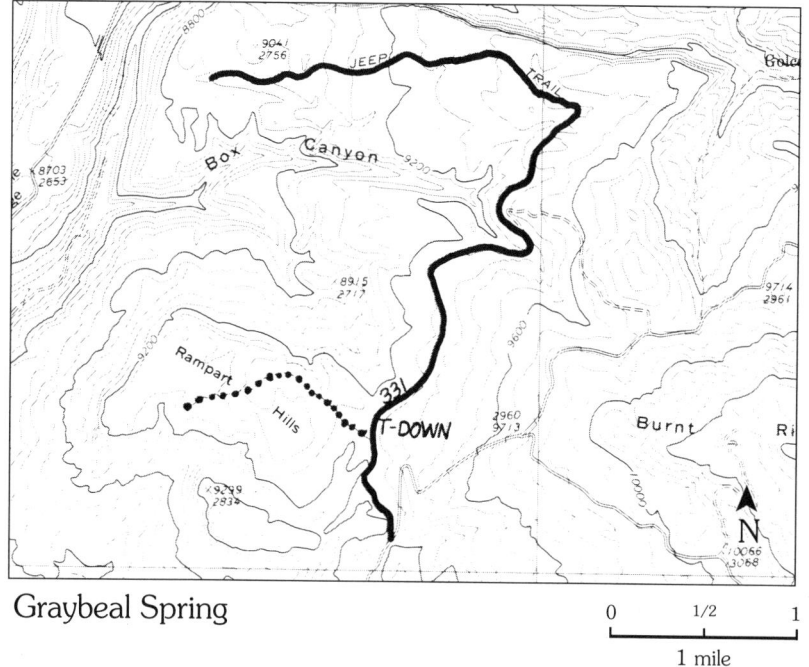

Graybeal Spring

Geology

Graybeal Spring is a point where groundwater seeps out from alluvium and the weathered Mancos Shale resting on the impervious igneous intrusion that forms the Rampart Hills. This type of spring is common on top of this intrusion. The trail to the spring stays on top of the sill-like mass and Mancos Shale residuum.

Coyote Park Loop

Distance: 12 miles (19 kilometers)

Difficulty: Very long and a lot of elevation gain on the way back to T-Down. The trail below the Ramparts can be rough and muddy during wet weather

Quadrangle: Rampart Hills

Time: 3 to 5 hours

Tips: Outrageous downhill to start—but watch for cars. Nice climb through beautiful country to return to T-Down

Elevation gain: 1,300 feet (396 meters)

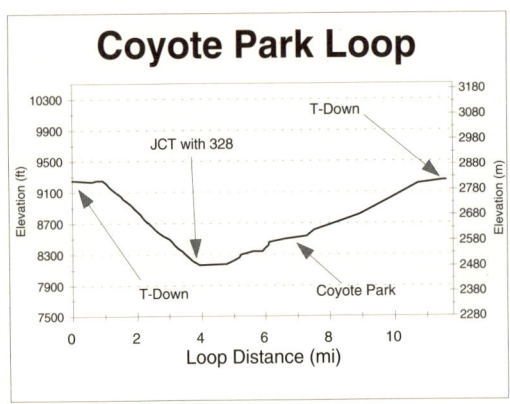

Description

Ride (or drive) down the main road (FS 331 to 566) for about four miles, to where a four-wheel-drive road (FS 328) takes off to the north (if you reach the second cattle guard, you've gone too far). This road leads off around the west side of the Rampart Hills for about 2.5 miles (4 kilometers) to where it splits into 328B and 328C. At about

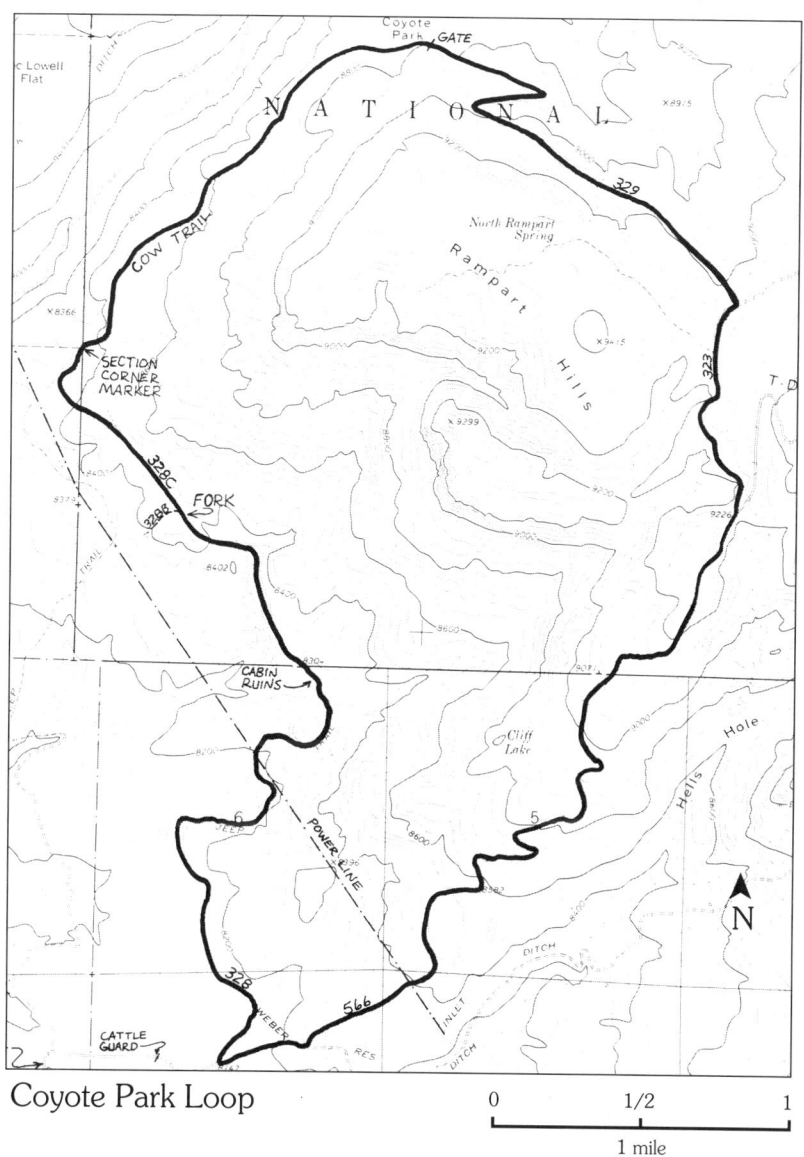

Coyote Park Loop

1.9 miles (3 kilometers) there are the ruins of an old cabin, probably a ranch of the late 1800s, built with a great view of the Rampart Hills. At about 5.5 miles (3.5 kilometers), you reach a gate opening onto land owned by the local school district. Proceed through this gate to the fork at 2.5 miles (4 kilometers). Take the right fork (FS 328C) and head around the Rampart Hills to the north. At about 3.5 miles (5.5 kilometers) the road becomes a trail and enters a grassy drainage area sometimes with a rather healthy congregation of bovines.

Keep climbing up the drainage to where it is apparent where the cows and others cross the little creek and advance toward the corner created by the intersection of two fence lines. This corner is also marked by a USGS survey point placed at the corners of sections on your quadrangle or Forest Service map. The sections are (clockwise starting in the upper left as indicated on the marker) S25, S30, S31, S36. There is a crude gate in the fence. Go through it and head up toward the Ramparts across a clearing until you reach some large scrub oaks. Here, a trail will take off to the left and climb up.

This trail leads on around the Ramparts on the edge of West Mancos Canyon, affording some great views, and winds through some large aspens. Between 4.5 and 5 miles (7 and 8 kilometers) the aspens have been logged and the trail starts to resemble a road. There are several deadfalls and water, and at 5.3 miles (8.5 kilometers) Coyote Park is reached. The Box Canyon trail takes off to the north, a short road splits the park, and the return road, FS 329, switches back and forth up the back side of the Ramparts toward T-Down. This road is in good shape and tops out, reaching FS 33, the Rampart Road, at 7.5 miles (12 kilometers). Shortly thereafter, T-Down is reached along with FS 566, which will take you back down to FS 328, if that is where you started. The entire loop is 12 miles (19 kilometers) and goes through beautiful country with added adventure on some truly remote trails.

Geology

Coyote Park is a level area on the Mancos Shale below the igneous intrusions of the Rampart Hills above, and just above the Dakota Sandstone. Some sandstone boulders on the soil are from sandstone beds in the Mancos Shale and from the transition zone between the Dakota Sandstone and the Mancos Shale.

Large aspen trees along the Coyote Park Trail.

Echo Basin Loop

Distance: 12.5 miles (20 kilometers)

Difficulty: Difficult due to elevation and climb. Road can be rocky.

Quadrangle: Rampart Hills

Time: 2 to 4 hours

Tips: Do you own Rock Shox?

Elevation gain: 1,387 feet (422 meters)

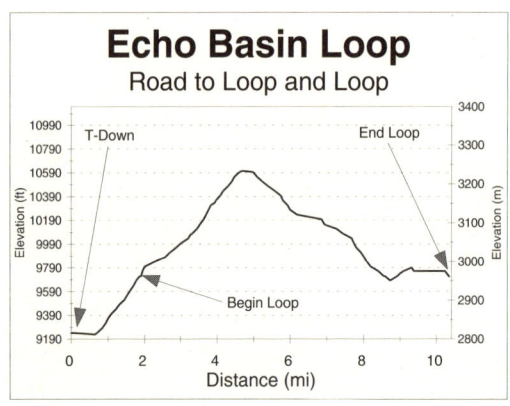

Description

From the junction of FS 331 and 566 (elevation 9,226 feet; 2,812 meters), climb up the main road for 2 miles (3.5 kilometers) to the turnoff to Echo Basin (elevation 9,713 feet; 2,961 meters). Take a right, staying on 566, and follow the road for about 2 miles (3.5 kilometers) to the turnoff to the top of Burnt Ridge. This is a nice side trip up to large beaver ponds (elevation 10,480 feet; 3,194 meters) with several large meadows. The main loop continues on up the canyon between Burnt Ridge to the north and the Hogback to the south, reaching its apex at about 4 miles (6.5 kilometers) at elevation

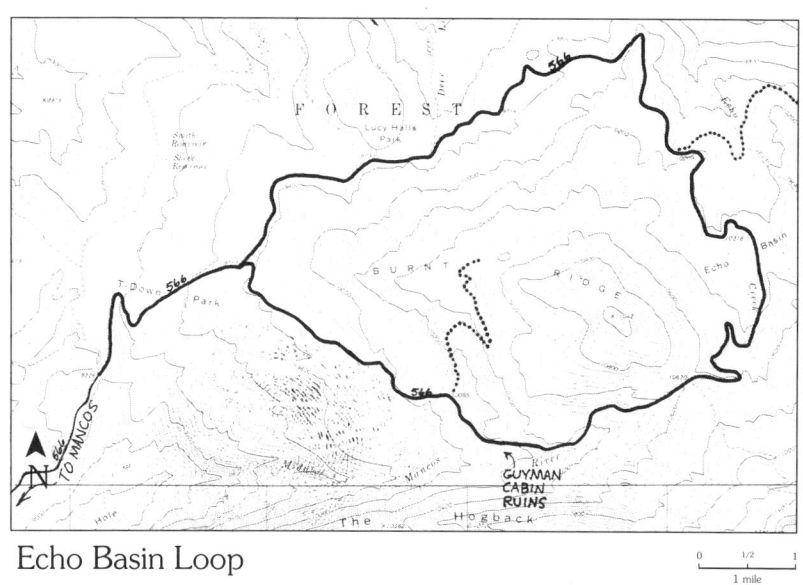

Echo Basin Loop

Making way along Echo Basin Road.

10,630 feet (3,240 meters), where a small logging road takes off to the right, another nice side trip to practice climbing at above 10,000 feet (3,048 meters). From here the road drops into Echo Basin (elevation 10,209 feet; 3,112 meters), and another side trip, a four-wheel-drive road leads up toward Owen Basin along the South Fork of the West Mancos River. From Echo Basin the road drops in elevation all the way back to where you turned right, then rapidly descends back to T-Down Park.

Geology

This ride makes a loop around Burnt Ridge, which is an igneous intrusion into the Mancos Shale. To the right on the way up is the Hogback, a long, narrow intrusion of similar material was emplaced around the same time, near the boundary between the Cretaceous and Tertiary periods. The rocky roads on the north side of the loop are composed of igneous and sandstone rocks transported down from above. There is a rock quarry on the road on the south side of Burnt Ridge that extracts the intrusive rocks supporting the mountain.

# The Hogback

Distance: 12 miles (19 kilometers) round trip
Difficulty: The climb is grueling
Quadrangle: Rampart Hills
Time: 2 to 4 hours
Tips: Outrageous downhill to start—but watch for cars. Serious climb through beautiful country to return to T-Down.
Elevation gain: 1,900 feet (579 meters)

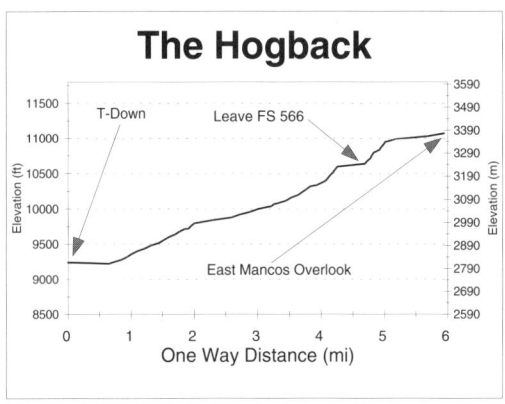

Description

Take the road east toward Echo Basin (FS 566) until you reach a junction at about 4.5 miles (7 kilometers). Take a right on FS 322 and climb up between the Hogback and Helmet Peak. At the saddle (elevation 10,951 feet; 3,338 meters), there is another trail that leads down the axis of the Hogback, and other roads that head off down into the Middle Mancos River and Silver Creek. There are some great views from the top of this large rock mass.

On the way up to the branch in the road at almost 3 miles (5 kilometers), note the overgrown ruins of Guyman Cabin off to the right. This cabin was built by settlers in the late 1800s and was kept up for many years before being abandoned and given to the national forest.

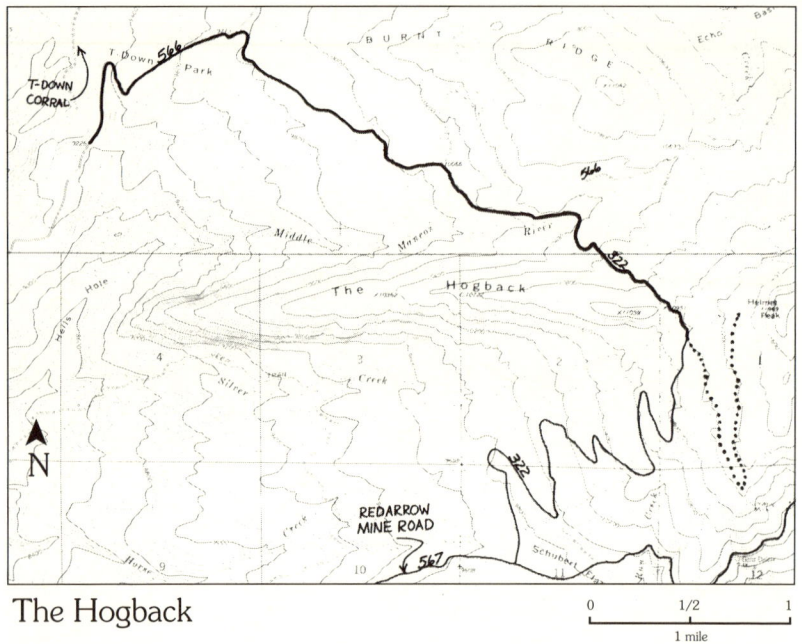

The Hogback

Geology

The side trip up on top of the Hogback leaves the Mancos Shale and climbs on top of a long, east-west trending intrusive body that squeezed and melted its way into a near-vertical east-west-trending fracture or fracture zone. Magma extended away from the intrusive core of the La Plata Mountains, then cooled rather quickly, fracturing vertically and at steep angles. From the south side of the Hogback the fractures are easily visible; on the north side the fractures are eroded to form large rock prominences. Above the Hogback is a large rock glacier formed by thousands of years worth of rock that has toppled down off the face of Helmet Peak, predominantly during times when the climate was much cooler than it is now.

As the talus got thicker and soil filled in the spaces between the angular boulders and cobbles, the entire mass began to move like a slow landslide, creating flow structures such as ridges and furrows in the surface. The slow rate of motion and bouldery surface has led researchers to refer to the masses as "rock glaciers."

The last reaches of the Hogback trail.

 **Millwood**

This old railroad station can be reached by taking Colorado 184 north out of Mancos toward Dolores for about 4 miles (6.5 kilometers), then taking a right on County Road 40 to Joe Moore Reservoir. After about 3 miles (4.5 kilometers), pass the turnoff to the reservoir and continue west, following the road as it winds to the north and Millwood.

There is adequate parking at Millwood, and a trail map for cross-country skiing is supplied by the Forest Service at the Mancos Ranger District office. The bike routes are the same as those for skiing and are relatively short and easy.

East Mancos River Drainage

The East Mancos River canyon is notorious for its rugged and remote terrain, although it is still geographically close to U.S. 160 and Mancos. Over the years the East Mancos canyon has provided good hunting and, before mineral constituents elevated around 1987, was a good, though tough to get to, fishing area. There is still some question whether the contamination was due to releases from the Gold Dollar Mine or was naturally elevated discharge from groundwater. It is not known when or if the system will ever return to normal.

The canyon is very deep and rugged and is flanked by Madden and Spiller Peaks, both of which can be climbed in an afternoon, and Madden Peak can be ridden most of the way to the summit. Trails in this section begin at one of two trailheads, and they can be shortened to decrease the difficulty rating. Several rides start at the junction of U.S. 160 and County Road 44, about 3 miles (5 kilometers) east of Mancos, and several start at the top of Mancos Hill, about 8 miles (13 kilometers) east of Mancos on U.S. 160. The trails on Menefee Mountain are not actually located in the East Mancos drainage but are included in this section anyway for simplicity.

The East Mancos River.

East Mancos Trails

Distance: Variable
Difficulty: Moderate
Quadrangle: La Plata, Thompson Park
Time: Variable
Tips: There are many trails to choose from
Elevation gain: 500–600 feet (152–183 meters) total relief

Description

About 2 miles (3.5 kilometers) up the Red Arrow Mine road (FS 567) from County Road 44, take a right on a four-wheel-drive road (FS 567D) at the Forest Service boundary and follow it along the side of the East Mancos River canyon. There are several different roads to choose from as you ride farther up the canyon, and you may eventually come to an outcrop of white limestone. There is no definite route for this ride, because there are so many ways you can ride it.

Geology

Most of this country is underlain by the Mancos Shale and Dakota Sandstone, but as you move up the canyon, you get into more and more of the Morrison Formation and, farther up, the Cutler Formation red beds. The south side of the canyon is underlain by the Junction Creek Sandstone, and along the bottom of the canyon is a thin outcrop of the Dolores Formation. The south end of the La Plata Mountains shows more of the effect of the uplift on the sedimentary beds as they dip off to the south, and the upper reaches have been glaciated down to as low as 9,200 feet (3,000 meters).

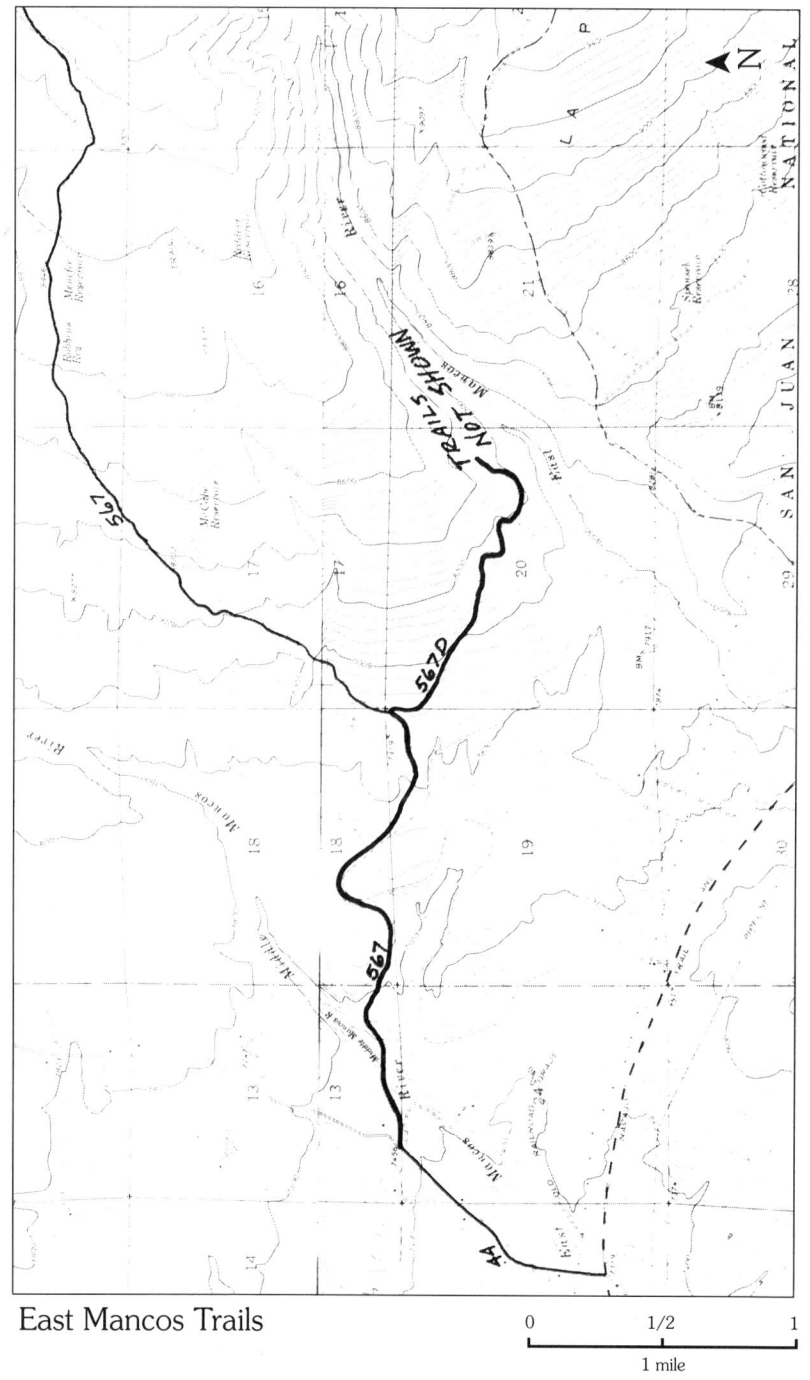

East Mancos Trails

Railroad Grade

Distance: 18.5 miles (30 kilometers) round trip
Difficulty: Easy, but can get muddy in rainstorms
Quadrangle: Thompson Park
Time: 2 hours to all day
Tips: This trail is a good ride or a good cross-country ski trail
Elevation gain: 460 feet (140 meters)

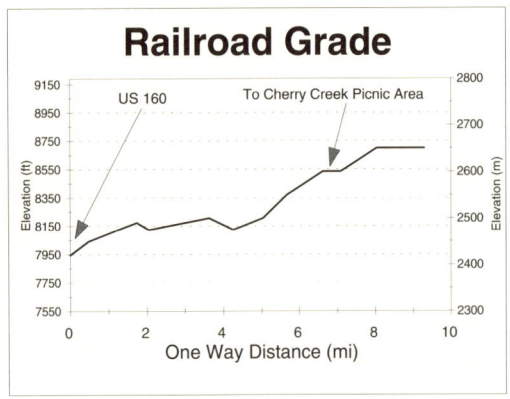

Description

The old railroad grade can be reached 8 miles (13 kilometers) east of Mancos, 1 mile (1.5 kilometers) north of U.S. 160 at the top of Mancos Hill on FS 316. Turn east on the grade just before a power line crosses the road. Follow the old Durango and Rio Grande Railroad route as it winds around the foothills above Thompson Park. The grade is easily rideable all the way to Cherry Creek (about 7 miles; 11.5 kilometers), and approximately 2 miles (3 kilometers) farther.

The grade is very gentle, as would be expected on a railroad route, and makes for a casual ride through the ponderosa and oak-brush forest.

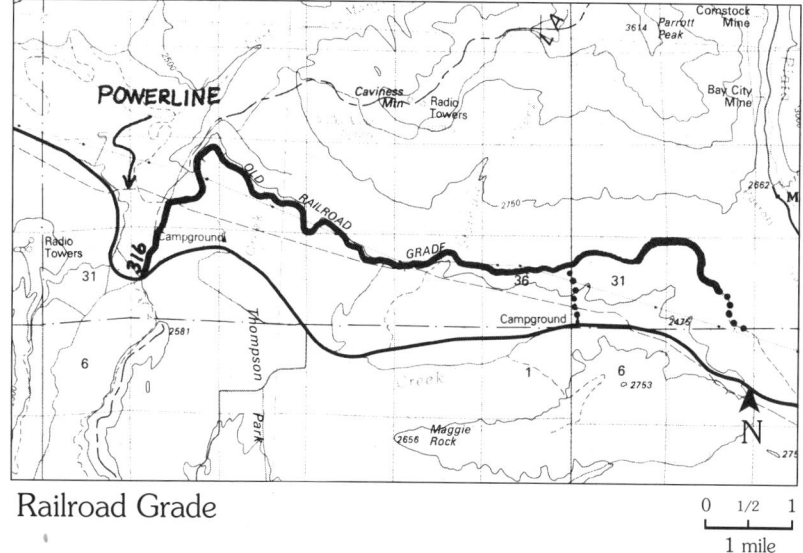

Railroad Grade

0 1/2 1
1 mile

This route offers great scenery during the September aspen and oak-brush color changes. Wildlife such as deer, elk, coyotes, and birds of prey are frequently sighted in this area.

If you can see south to where Cherry Creek drains the park, you will see the general location of th ranch where the late western author Louis L'Amour lived for years. This park has been a favorite of many ranching families over the years because of the higher elevation, which brings more precipitation and good grazing during the summer months.

Geology

As mentioned, the railroad grade is on the lower Mancos Shale with little variation. To the south in Thompson Park, outcrops of the Mesa Verde Formation support cliffs left as the slopes retreat to the south.

Rush Basin

Distance: 20 miles (32 kilometers) round trip

Difficulty: Hard; extreme elevation gain; rocky but not that technical

Quadrangle: Thompson Park, Rampart Hills, La Plata

Time: 5 hours

Tips: This ride is through nice scenery and into a historic basin, but it is grueling; not for beginners

Elevation gain: 4,200 feet (1,280 meters)

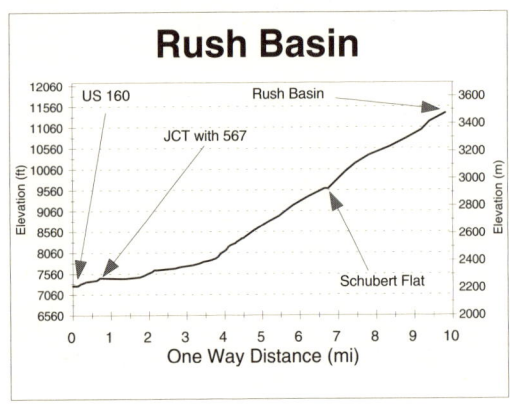

Description

From the Echo Basin road (County Road 44) junction with U.S. 160 (elevation 7,319 feet; 2,230 meters), about three miles east of Mancos, head up toward Echo Basin past the Reddert Ranch on the south side of the road and the old Menefee cabin. About 1 mile (1.5 kilometers) up this road, take a right on the Red Arrow Mine road (FS 567) and drop down to the Middle Mancos River. Climb out of the Middle Mancos River valley for about four miles to a branch in the road (elevation 8,946 feet; 2,728 meters) where FS 325 heads north toward Silver Creek; bear right, staying on 567, and climb for about

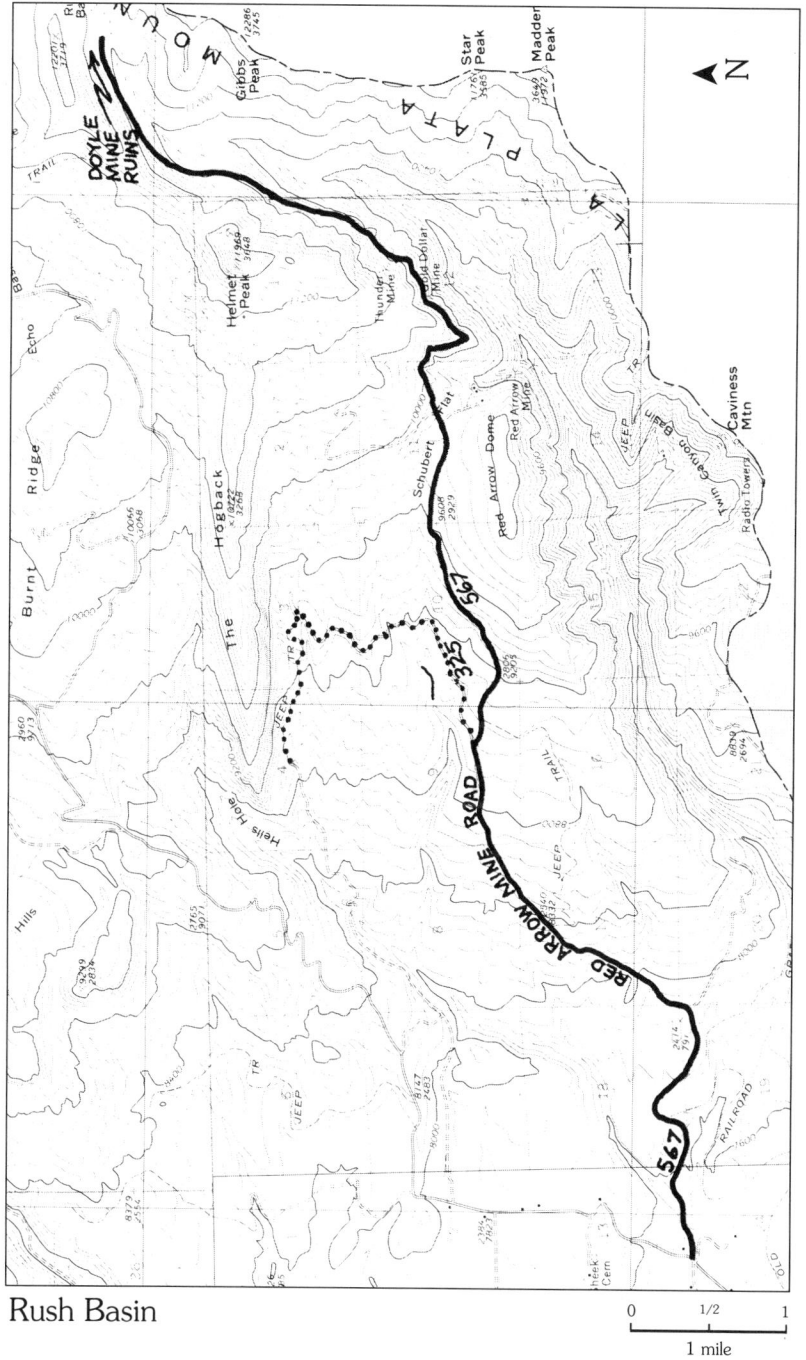

Rush Basin

2.5 miles (4 kilometers) to Schubert Flat, named for the miner who died from injuries sustained in a mine just north of here. Continue straight on up until you cross Gold Run Creek. At this point you can look down for over 1,000 feet (300 meters) to the East Mancos River, which was polluted by acid and mineral groundwater in 1987 and is still considered "dead." The road continues on up the side of the canyon for about 3.5 miles (5.5 kilometers) to Rush Basin (elevation 11,800 feet; 3,597 meters), and remember, as you look up at Spiller Peak, that it's all downhill, albeit rough, back to the car.

The Doyle Mine ruins are still standing in Rush Basin. A huge snow avalanche wiped out most of the workings, killing six people, in 1936. There are other prospects, as well, in the East Mancos canyon, because this was one of the most profitable mining areas in this otherwise low-grade region. The road that led you to Rush Basin is around one hundred years old and probably looked very different when it was first constructed. Climatological studies have shown that timberline was at a lower elevation in those times, and the growing season was shorter and cooler. Winter precipitation was probably also greater.

This climb is of a very high elevation over a rough road, so extra water should be carried. At Rush Basin it is possible to reach the East Mancos River for water, but between the top and bottom there are only a pair of intermittent streams, and neither can be counted on for water.

A shorter trip on this ride is to take the turn at FS 325 and head into the Silver Creek basin. This road winds around and climbs a bit more before dropping into the Middle Mancos River valley along the south side of the Hogback. This trail is pretty rough and is closed when it reaches private land. Still another variation is to take FS 322 up toward Helmet Peak. This is a serious climb but could also be a fun loop ride because it is all downhill back to T-Down via FS 566, and from there back to the head of the Red Arrow Mine road, FS 567, and U.S. 160.

Geology

The climb out of the Mancos River Valley crosses the active floodplain, climbing immediately onto older river terraces. Forest Service 567 drops back down onto the active floodplain of the Middle Mancos River and then climbs up onto old cobbled and graveled terraces formed by outwash from glaciers around thirty thousand years old or older. After entering the national forest, the road leaves the younger deposits and climbs up over the bedding planes of the Dakota Sandstone exposed during excavation for the road. These beds have been tilted by the laccolithic intrusion of the La Plata Mountains. The highest point on the initial climb is Red Arrow Dome, which is near the boundary between the sedimentary units and the igneous intrusions. Near the intrusions, the rocks are fractured and enriched with minerals, and thus we have the mines. Past Schubert Flat, the road crosses the divide into the East Mancos canyon, the east side of which is underlain by the Cutler Formation that forms the red beds coloring the valley north of Durango.

The road then crosses the Morrison Formation and a thin exposure of the Junction Creek Sandstone. The last several miles of the ride cross slide rock that has toppled down from the Dakota Sandstone and Morrison Formation, and igneous rocks that make up Helmet Peak. The color that flanks the bottoms of Spiller, Burwell, and Gibbs Peaks indicates mineralization and intrusive rocks that are common in Rush Basin.

 # Madden Peak

Distance: 8 miles (13 kilometers) round trip
Difficulty: Hard due to considerable elevation gain
Quadrangle: Thompson Park, Hesperus, La Plata
Time: 5 to 7 hours
Tips: Major climb and rough roads. Good climb for training.
Elevation gain: 3,070 feet (936 meters)

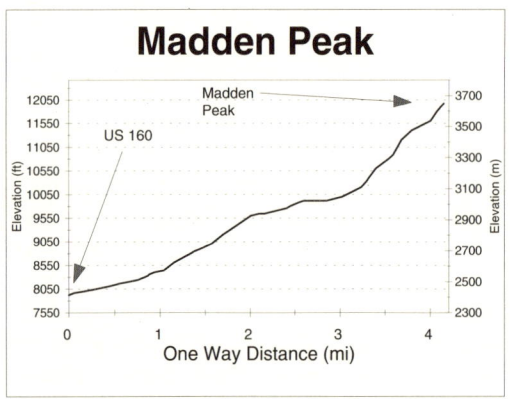

Description

From the top of Mancos Hill (elevation 7,930 feet; 2,417 meters), about 5 miles (8 kilometers) east of Mancos on U.S. 160, head north on FS 316. Climb up the rocky four-wheel-drive road for about seven miles to an old prospect at the head of East Gulch at elevation 11,000 feet (3,352 meters). There is a trail that will take you near the summit of Madden Peak, depending on how much energy you have left and the weather conditions. Most of the climb is over four-wheel-drive roads, but be careful of ruts that can send you flying off into the oak brush.

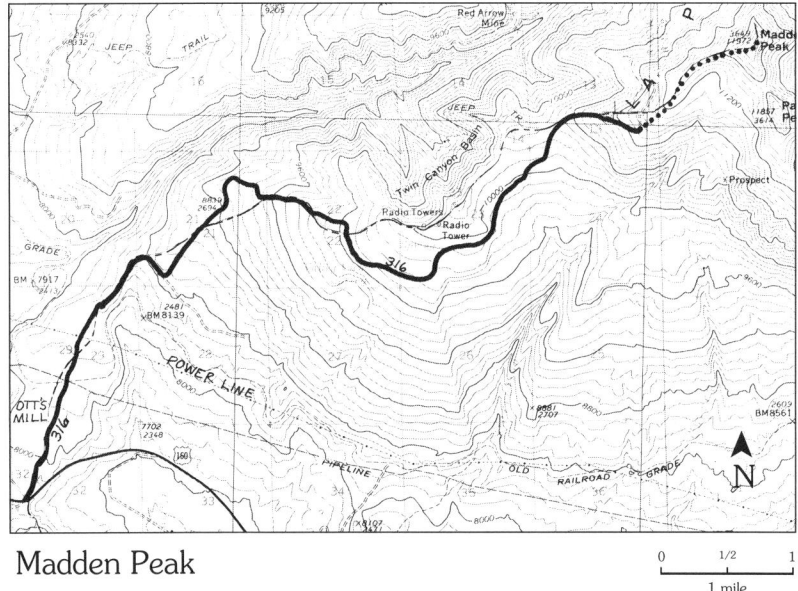

Madden Peak

Geology

The first several kilometers travel over a fluvial deposit washed out of the mountains during an older glacial cycle before the current East Mancos canyon was cut. Leaving the rocky soil, you climb across the Mancos Shale for about 1.25 miles (2 kilometers) before climbing on top of the Dakota Sandstone. The trail crosses the Morrison Formation and Junction Creek Sandstone, which is very hard due to the thermal effects of the intruding magma below. There is an intrusion to the east of the trail that cannot be seen, and two faults in the Junction Creek Sandstone near the top of the peak. The prospect in East Gulch did not profit from ore in this area, probably because of the location near these two faults. Faults can often provide plumbing to enrich the rocks with minerals, but these faults where not hooked up to anything significant, such as the fractures that run from La Plata Canyon into the East Mancos canyon.

Menefee Peak

Distance: 5.5 miles (9 kilometers) round trip
Difficulty: Moderate
Quadrangle: Thompson Park, Mancos
Time: 2 to 3 hours
Tips: Watch out for motor vehicles
Elevation gain: 904 feet (275 meters)

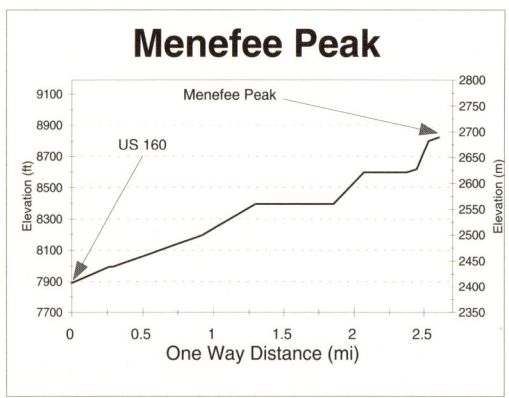

Description

Near the west edge of Mancos Hill, 8 miles (13 kilometers) east of Mancos on U.S 160, a four-wheel-drive road takes off to the southwest and winds up Menefee Mountain to a set of radio towers located on top of Menefee Peak. It overlooks Mancos, East Canyon, and lands to the west and south. The road is in relatively good shape most of the time and is not that technical by mountain-bike standards, but there is a caterpillar-track firebreak along the top of Menefee Mountain for a good distance to the south. This can certainly provide some challenging and truly off-road riding.

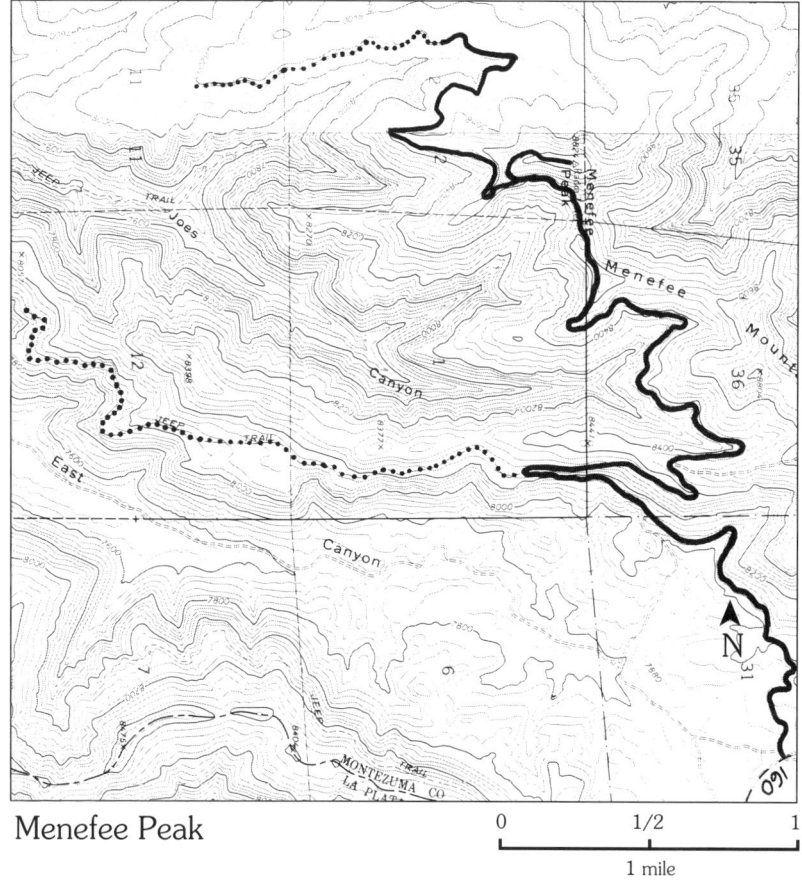

Menefee Peak

 Wildlife is common on this trail, including deer, elk, mountain lion, and bear, all of which have been sighted on the road. The vegetation is predominantly oak brush, which is nice because it does not block your view of the surrounding country, and there are clumps of ponderosa pine on peaks and ridges, and aspens in draws.
 It should be noted that there is another trail to the towers on the east side of East Canyon, as well. This is a good climb with the same types of vistas, as well as coal mines.

Unexpected company on Menefee Mountain.

Geology

The trail starts on the edge of glacial outwash from glacial advances during the Quaternary period. The road quickly leaves this material and climbs into the Mesa Verde Group, which supports Menefee Mountain. The sandstone-cliff-forming beds are of the Point Lookout Sandstone, and the shale beds with seams of coal are the Menefee Formation and can be located by the presence of numerous abandoned mines. The Mesa Verde Group dips off to the south-southeast, away from the La Plata Mountains and toward the San Juan Basin. Far off in the distance, if the pollution from the Four Corners coal power plants isn't too thick, you can see the San Juan Basin.

La Plata Canyon

The mouth of La Plata Canyon is on U.S. Highway 160 about 13 miles (21 kilometers) west of Durango, or 16 miles (26 kilometers) east of Mancos near the turnoff to Hesperus, which is south of the highway. La Plata County Road 124 takes off to the north toward the small historic town of Mayday (4 miles; 6.5 kilometers). Rides in this section can all be found from Mayday. Kroeger Campground is a Forest Service campground just north of Mayday.

La Plata Canyon is a rather linear, steep-walled canyon that drains the east side of the mountains described in previous chapters. Relief is as much as 3,300 feet (1,000 meters), and each side canyon is very steep. The area is rich in mining history, containing the Gold King Mill and the town of La Plata. Virtually every trail in the canyon is related to mining from some time in the past. The trails described here may not be suitable for everyone because they tend to climb very steeply for thousands of feet to a mine and then return. As mentioned, these trails are very good for training in climbing at altitude. Some of the trails are somewhat technical because of their rocky nature; the Mancos Shale is not present in this canyon. Most of the rocks present in La Plata Canyon are monzanites and syenites of the La Plata igneous core. There are also some metamorphosed sedimentary rocks near the bottom of the canyon.

The La Plata Canyon mining district turned out to be more productive than the prospects closer to Mancos, and a couple of the operations are still running around Snowstorm Peak. Around 1874, the towns of La Plata, Mayday, and Parrott City were thriving and counting on La Plata Canyon mining to deliver large profits. Speculators from Mancos and Durango invested in mines there, and the town of Hesperus sprang up as trade and travel headed south toward Fort Lewis and the San Juan River settlements.

This area never prospered, though Parrott City was planned by real-estate investors to become the county seat of La Plata County.

Cyclists at the head of La Plata Canyon.

Investors purchased three hundred acres from Chief Ignacio of the Ute tribe, who at the time still held claim to that area. But the geologic setting doomed La Plata Canyon to a life of low-grade ore and speculation. The La Plata Mountains were produced by shallow intrusives, bringing mineral-rich fluids into surrounding rocks through fracture conduits. But the amount of enrichment was very limited and pales in comparison to the huge volcanic eruptions that took place at Silverton and Creede during the Tertiary period, which produced the rich deposits at Savage Basin and Camp Bird between Telluride and Ouray.

# Cumberland Basin

Distance: 18 miles (29 kilometers) round trip
Difficulty: Hard: long and continuous climb, but few technical sections
Quadrangle: Hesperus, La Plata
Time: 2 to 5 hours
Tips: Be ready for a long climb and fast descent
Elevation gain: 2,885 feet (879 meters)

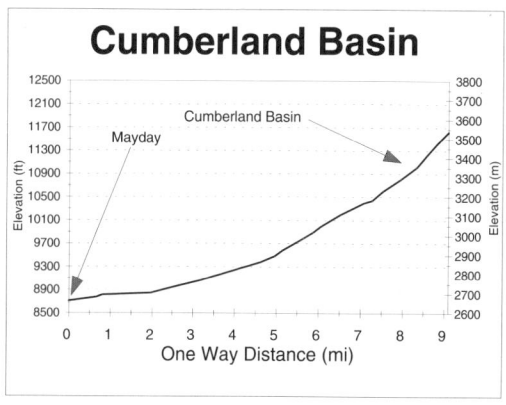

Description

From the historic mining town of Mayday (elevation 8,735 feet; 2,662 meters), ride north on La Plata County Road 124 past another historic town, La Plata (about 6 miles, or 9.5 kilometers), and on up the canyon for a total of 10 miles (16 kilometers) to Cumberland Basin (elevation 11,620 feet; 3,542 meters). Along the way, the Gold King Mill is located at about 7 miles (11 kilometers), and the Cumberland Mine ruins are near the top at about 9 miles (15 kilometers) from Mayday. The other trails described here also take off to the right and left on the way up the canyon, and peaks rise up above the steep canyon walls.

From the top of the canyon, several other trails are accessible. The Kenebec Pass road/trail leads over the east divide to Lightner

Cumberland Basin

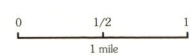

Creek, the Colorado Trail, and eventually Durango. The trail to the west leads over the opposite divide to Bear Creek Basin and eventually Sharkstooth Pass. A trail to the north leads off into Hermosa Creek.

Geology

This ride travels up the long, linear canyon, glaciated down to about 9,840 feet (3,000 meters) during at least the last glaciation (until fifteen thousand years ago). The road is mostly on the Cutler Formation, which is intruded by igneous dikes. The last 3 miles (5 kilometers) before Cumberland Basin is into the core of the La Plata laccolith, and most of the bedrock is monzanite and syenite. As you climb up over the top to look down into Hermosa and Bear Creeks, you will see large glaciated valleys with red and gray beds of the Cutler and Hermosa Formations forming the walls of the canyons similar to those seen north of Durango.

Another thing to note as you ride up the canyon is the condition of the La Plata River and the tributaries that run under the road. Madden Creek, about 1 mile (1.5 kilometers) from Kroeger Campground is relatively full of life, with algae on rocks and aquatic insects reproducing, while Bedrock Creek (about half a mile farther north) is dead. Bedrock Creek drains a heavily mined basin above, and the channel consists of bare rocks and no aquatic life. About 1 mile later, Boren Creek is much richer with life because it drains a basin that was mined less, and there are fewer naturally occurring minerals in the groundwater seeping into the creek.

A recent mine cuts into Cumberland Basin.

# Allard Mine

Distance: 9 miles (14.5 kilometers) round trip
Difficulty: Hard: some technical stretches, very steep and continuous climb
Quadrangle: La Plata
Time: 1 to 3 hours
Tips: Be ready for an intense climb and radical descent
Elevation gain: 1,793 feet (547 meters)

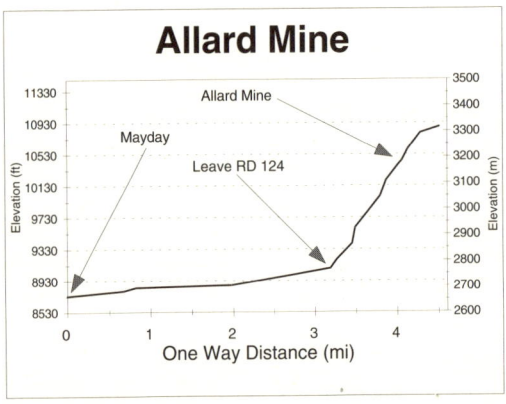

Description

About 3.1 miles (5.0 kilometers) north of Mayday (elevation 9,087 feet; 2,770 meters), turn left on FS 344 and head up the rocky four-wheel-drive road up the side of the canyon. The road traverses the valley wall until it reaches the Allard Mine and its reddish brown iron precipitate coating the ground in front of the portal. The road switches back to the south just before the mine, and, taking that route, you will be at 10,880 feet (3,316 meters) looking out across the San Juan Basin to the south, about 2 miles (3.5 kilometers) from County Road 124. This mine is relatively young, and it may or may not be worked now, but looking out across Bedrock Creek you can see the impact of mineralization and mining over the last century.

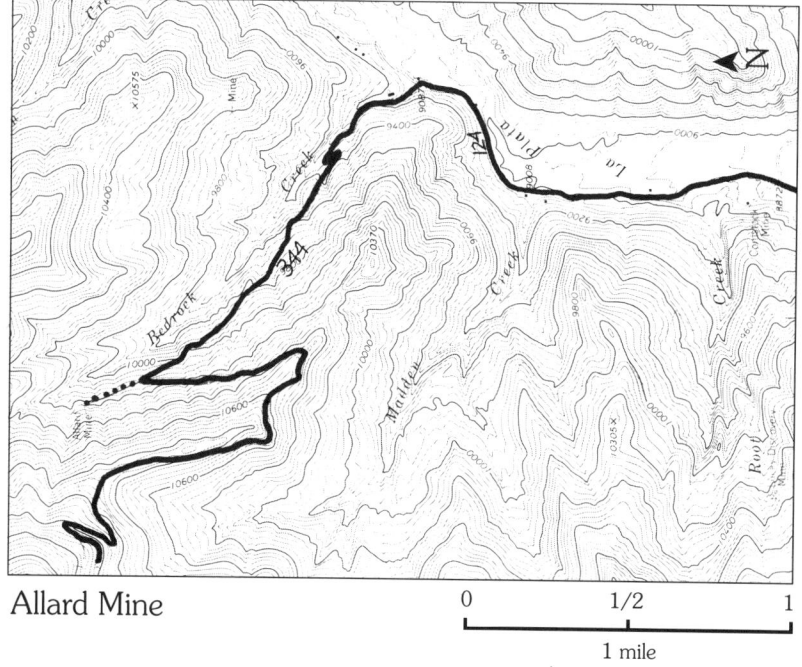

Allard Mine

0   1/2   1

1 mile

This area was never mined by a large operation, as were the Camp Bird or Tomboy Mines, of historical significance in the San Juans near Telluride and Ouray, yet it is obvious how the fragile subalpine environment here has been affected.

Geology

This climb travels over the Permian Cutler Formation, which has been baked by intruding magma. Intrusive rocks can be seen along the way, especially around the mine itself. Bedrock Creek is aptly named because nearly all the topsoil has been removed during mining in the drainage. The creek is also devoid of life because of mineral drainage, some from natural fracture outcrops, but mostly from mines like the Allard, as can be seen in the thick deposit of iron and magnesium at the mine portal, where water drains unrestricted. On the other side of the divide is the East Mancos drainage and several of the more profitable local mines, enriched by the same fractures that brought the minerals to this area.

# Boren Creek

Distance: 13 miles (21 kilometers) round trip
Difficulty: Hard: some technical stretches, very steep and continuous climb
Quadrangle: La Plata
Time: 1 to 3 hours
Tips: Be ready for an intense climb and radical descent
Elevation gain: 1,960 feet (597 meters)

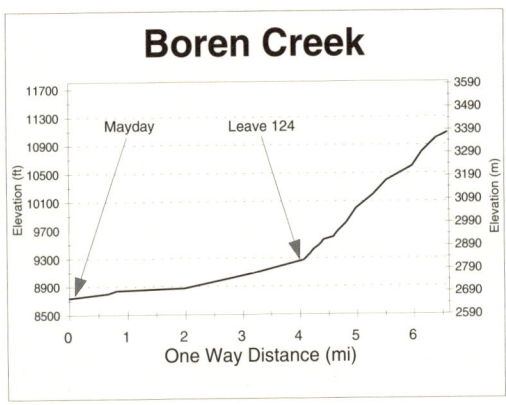

Description

About 4 miles (6.5 kilometers) north of Mayday on County Road 124, turn left at the junction with FS 061 (elevation 9,280 feet; 2,829 meters) and head up the side of the canyon. This trail zigzags up Boren Creek for about 2 miles (3.5 kilometers) to elevation 11,240 feet (3,426 meters). This is an intense climb through the timber to a point where you can look up at Burwell, Spiller, and Babcock Peaks.

Geology

This trail climbs rapidly over intrusive monzanites and syenites of the La Plata laccolith. There were several prospects in this area that

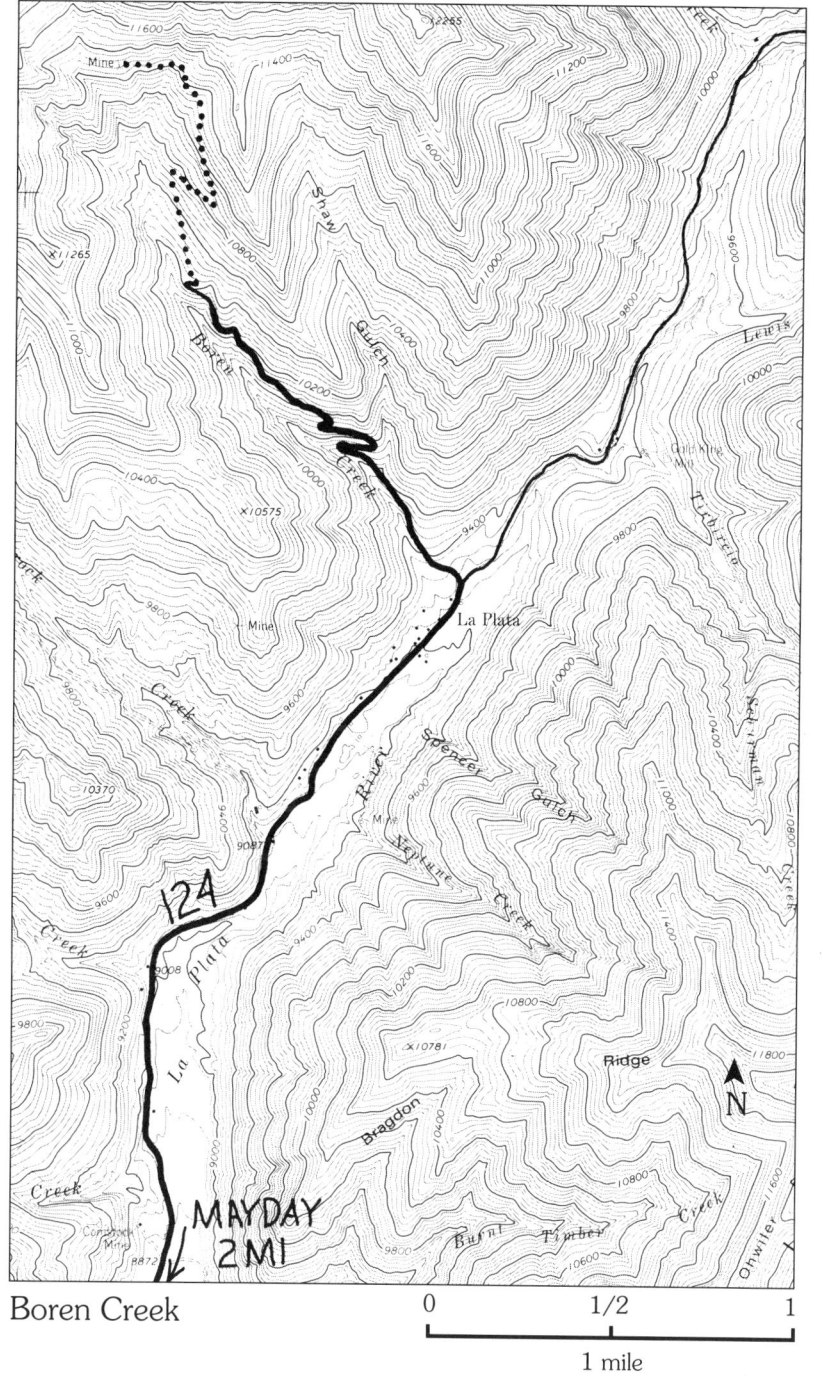
Boren Creek

attempted to tap into enriched zones, but they never panned out. It is apparent here how variable the mineral enrichment is in the La Platas, because the Bedrock Creek drainage is much more heavily mineral-laden, and hence more heavily mined.

 # Eagle Pass

Distance: 7 miles (11 kilometers)
Difficulty: Very hard: somewhat technical, very steep and continuous climb
Quadrangle: La Plata
Time: 3 to 5 hours
Tips: Be ready for an intense climb and radical descent
Elevation gain: 2,336 feet (766 meters)

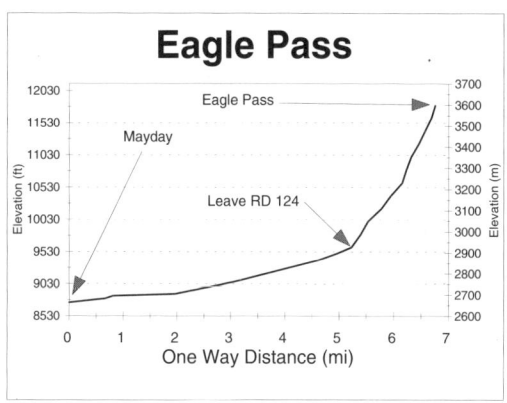

Description

Take a right on FS 060, a four-wheel-drive road (junction at elevation 9,440 feet; 2,877 meters) that climbs up Lewis Creek, leaving County Road 124 about 5 miles (8 kilometers) north of Mayday. This road climbs very steeply for the first mile, then climbs a bit more gradually for another mile, then switchbacks to the top of the ridge, wrapping around the south side of an unnamed peak just south of Eagle Pass (elevation 11,776 feet; 3,590 meters). On the east side of the ridge are several mines, but the road over the top does not lead anywhere.

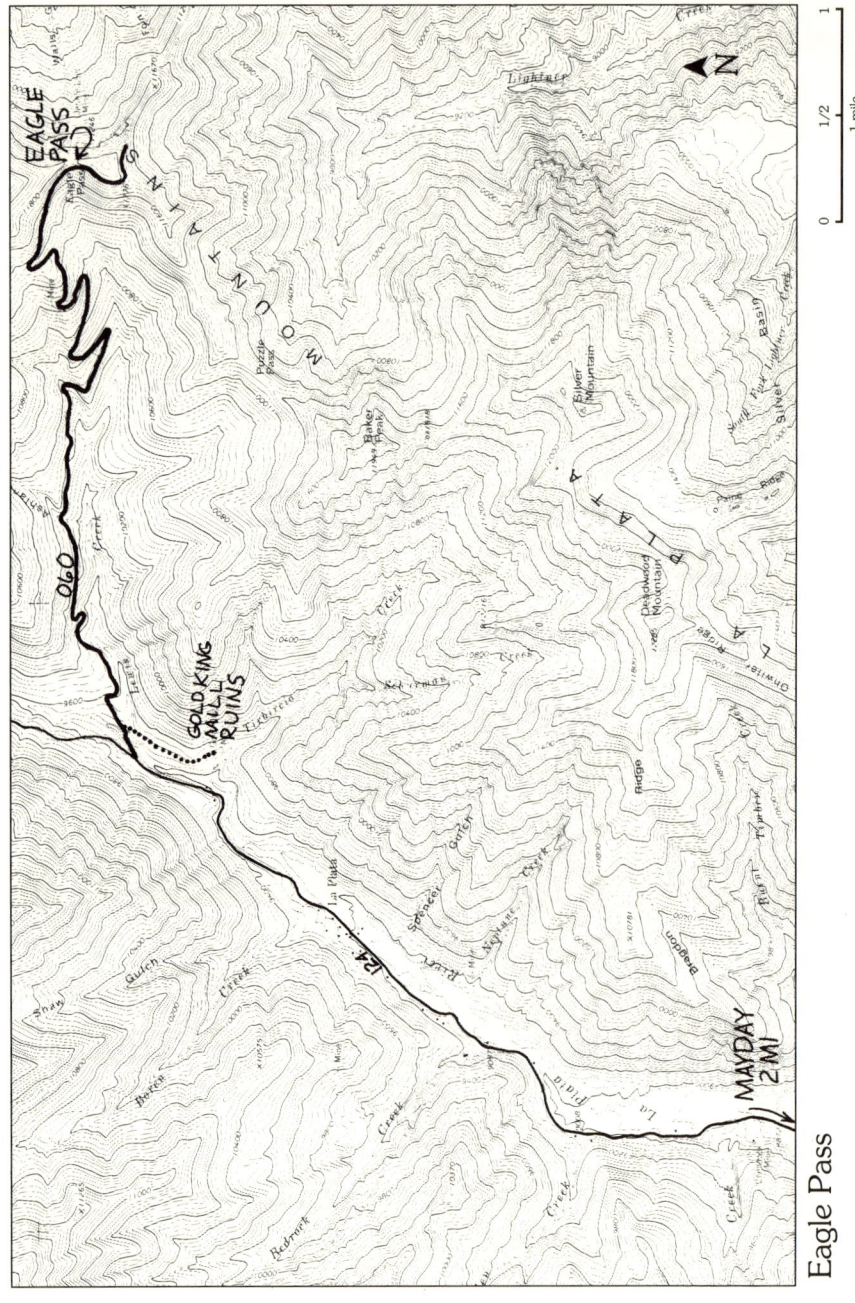

Gold King Mill, seen along a side trip from Eagle Pass.

On the way up from County Road 124 there is a short side trip along the La Plata River to the Gold King Mill ruins. The old road takes off to the right from FS 060 just after crossing the La Plata River. You will have to cross a small chasm just off the right side of the road, and it is good to have a riding partner to help handle the bikes. The chasm is only about eight or ten feet deep, but it has steep sides formed by the Lewis Creek cutting through the igneous rock. Past Lewis Creek, it is a relatively easy half-mile ride to the mill ruins. The mill processed ore from mines up the canyon, such as the Allard and Tomahawk Mines, and then the ore was sent on to Durango smelters. The ruins consist of weathered timbers and concrete foundations with much of the structure still intact.

Geology

This trail climbs to the top of the divide between the La Plata River and Lightner Creek to the east. If you aren't too bleary, you might notice several sill-like intrusions in the Permian Cutler Formation that makes up this whole side of the massif.

Tomahawk Mine

Distance: 13.5 miles (22 kilometers) round trip
Difficulty: Hard: some parts very technical, very steep climb
Quadrangle: La Plata
Time: 1 hour
Tips: Be ready for an intense climb and radical descent
Elevation gain: 1,200 feet (366 meters)

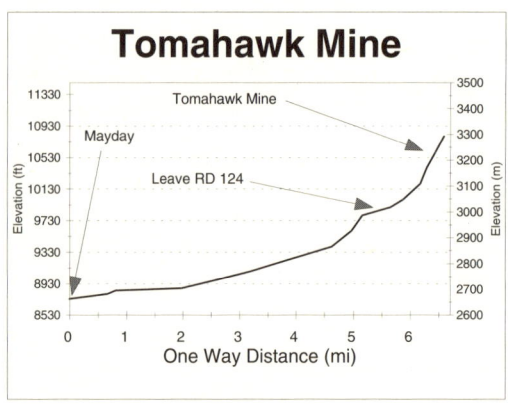

Description

About 6.5 miles (10 kilometers) north of Mayday (elevation 9,880 feet; 3,011 meters), a four-wheel-drive road leaves County Road 124, cutting back to the south toward Basin Creek. It climbs up the creek, zigzagging for about 1.25 miles (2 kilometers), becoming rougher and rougher, to the remnants of the Tomahawk Mine. The trail continues on for another quarter-mile past the remnants of the Little Kate Mine, then ends at an unnamed prospect at 11,080 feet (3,377 meters) elevation. There are no guarantees as to how rideable the trail is after the first 1.5 miles or so.

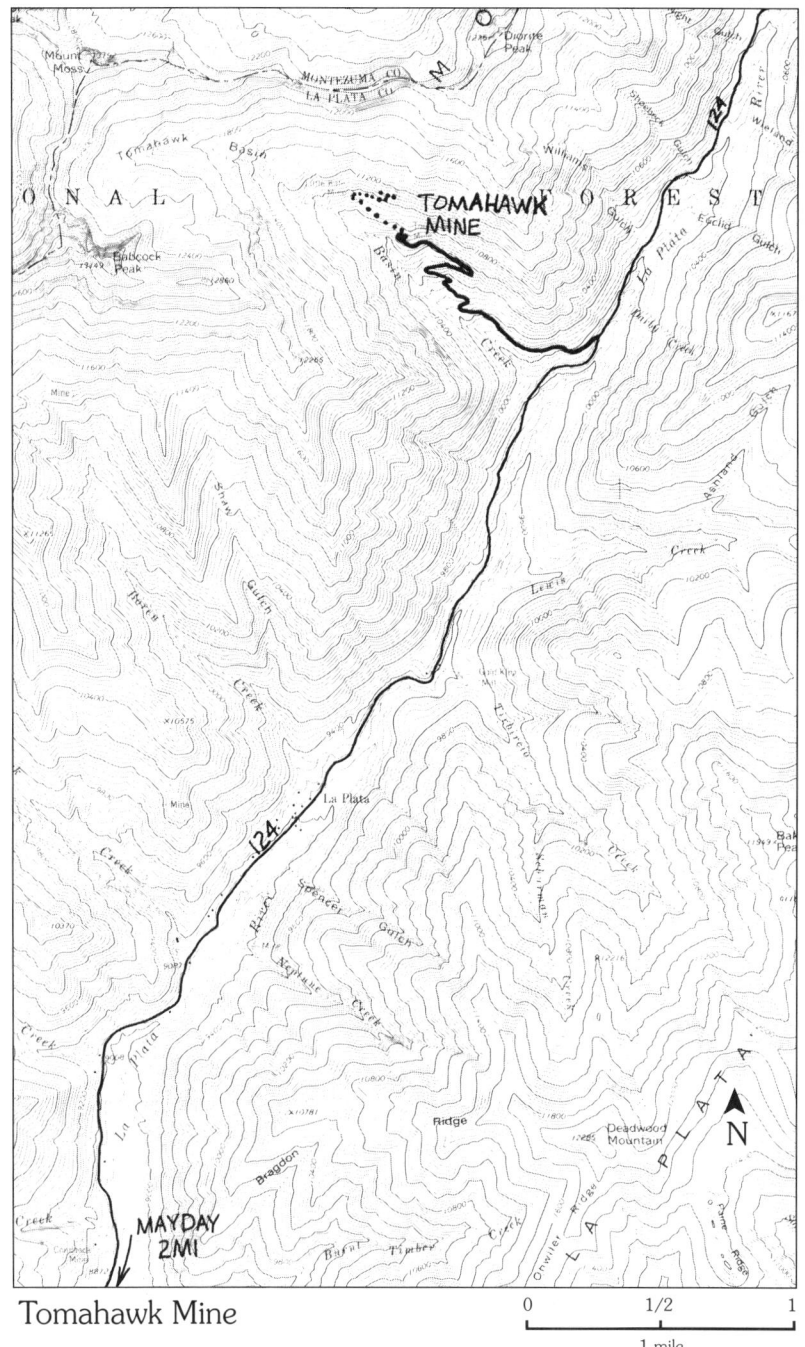

Tomahawk Mine

Geology

The geology of this ride is almost entirely on the top of a shallow laccolith at the heart of the La Plata Mountains. This is evident in the hard igneous rocks covering the roadbed. To the east you can see the large mining tracts around the bottom of Lewis Mountain, including the Columbus Basin mines that are still being worked.

 Snowstorm Peak Loop

Distance: 18 miles (29 kilometers) total, with loop
Difficulty: Very hard: long climbs, large elevation gains, and technical rocky trail at high elevation
Quadrangle: La Plata
Time: 5 to 6 hours
Tips: True high-altitude technical riding, and a firsthand look at current mining operations
Elevation gain: 2,820 feet (860 meters) from County Road 124

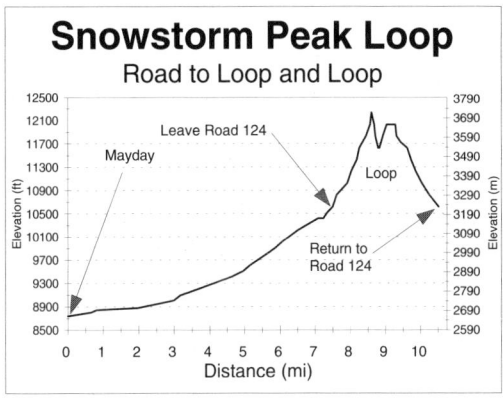

Description

About 7.5 miles (12 kilometers) north of Mayday (junction elevation 10,480 feet 3,194 kilometers) on County Road 124, the road to the Columbus Mine takes off to the east and climbs up Columbus Creek. The road continues on past the Columbus Mine, and this area may cause access problems if the mine is in operation. Continue climbing up past the mine to Columbus Basin, a nicely carved glacial cirque with a small cirque lake. From here the trail climbs up over the ridge the road drops steeply to the Bessy G Mine, then traverses the slope, cuts through a notch, and drops into another beautiful glacial

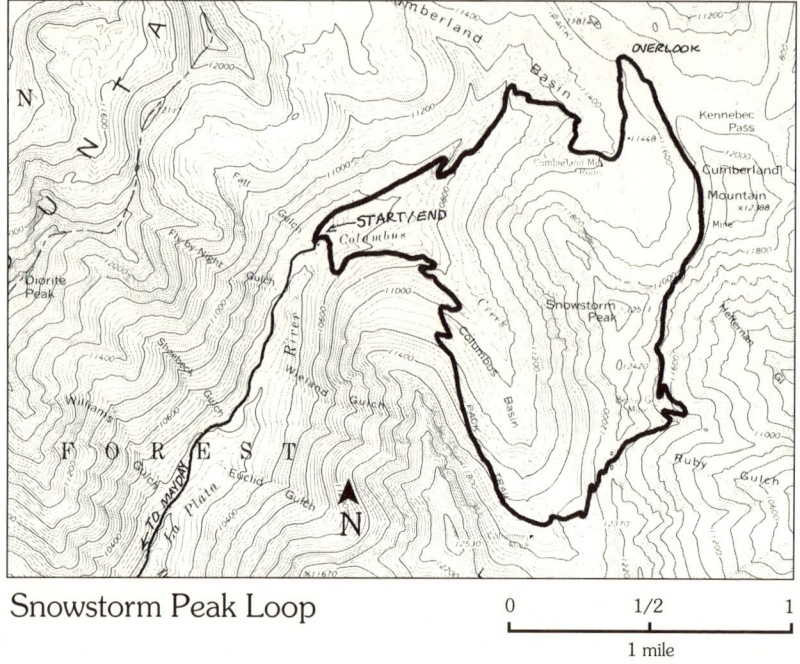

Snowstorm Peak Loop

cirque and Cumberland Basin. In Cumberland Basin, take the main road back down to the starting point, completing the loop around Snowstorm Peak.

This loop can be made easier by parking a car at the beginning of the loop and driving another to Cumberland Basin to begin at the top. This cuts out about 1,200 feet (367 meters) of climbing but still provides great views and technical riding on the rocky terrain above timberline.

Geology

Snowstorm Peak is supported by altered Cutler Formation with dikes intruding into the south side. This location is at the heart of mineral enrichment in the La Platas, as seen in the continuing operations in Columbus Basin and at the Bessie G Mine on the east side. These locations were not workable in the early days of mining history because of the high elevation and type of ore extracted, which could not be processed at the Durango smelters economically. There are ruins of the Cumberland Mine in Cumberland Basin, where operations were attempted around the turn of the century.

Climbing toward Columbus Basin on the way to Snowstorm Peak.

McPhee Reservoir

McPhee Reservoir is located just west of the town of Dolores, created by the Bureau of Reclamation by an embankment dam (Dolores Dam) on the Dolores River. There are several rides to the east and west of the reservoir that are for the most part moderate in difficulty and not very technical. The Dolores River canyon is picturesque, possibly one of the best in the state, and below the Dolores Dam the river cuts a deep canyon as it crosses western Colorado toward the Colorado River, joining it upstream from Moab, Utah.

McPhee is also rather picturesque and provides good fishing and waterskiing. From the Mancos area, take Colorado 184 for 20 miles (30 kilometers) to the junction with Colorado 145. To reach trails to the east of the reservoir, take a right and drop into the Dolores River valley and the town of Dolores. A left turn in the middle of town takes you north to FS 526 after climbing up and across the side of the canyon wall, then turning north. The national forest boundary is reached in about 3.5 miles (5.5 kilometers), and in about 7 miles (11 kilometers) you will reach FS 529, which takes off to the left. Park at the intersection.

To reach the rides west of the reservoir, turn left at the junction of highways 184 and 145 and travel west for 1 mile (1.5 kilometer) to another junction. Take a right on County Road 27, continuing past the Anasazi Heritage Center and other turnoffs to McPhee and Narraguinnep Reservoir, where the road becomes Colorado 184 again, and onto U.S. Highway 666 at Roundup Junction. Take a right here northward to Dove Crek. In about 10.5 miles (16.5 kilometers), take a right on FS 505. In almost exactly 1 mile (1.6 kilometers), the road turns north for 2.75 miles (4.5 kilometers), where it turns right again, dropping into the Dolores River canyon. Park at Bradford Bridge.

Camping is available at the House Creek Campground east of McPhee, and at Bradfield, Cabin Canyon, and Ferris Canyon Campgrounds to the west.

House Creek Area

Distance: 6 miles (9.5 kilometers)
Difficulty: Moderate
Quadrangle: Trimble Point, Boggy Draw
Time: 2 to 3 hours
Tips: Take lots of water
Elevation gain: 660 feet (200 meters)

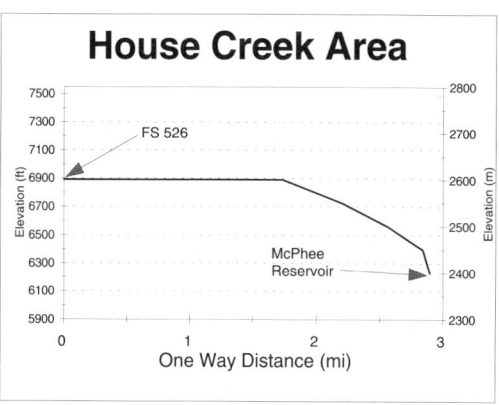

Description

Take FS 526 out of downtown Dolores up out of the Dolores River valley for about 10 miles (16 kilometers) past the turnoff to the House Creek boat ramp (FS 528). After the turnoff, the road climbs up out of House Creek to the turnoff to the left, to FS 529. Park along 529 and ride west over hills and swales through the ponderosa forest. The first gate is at about 1.5 miles (2.5 kilometers), and it is 2 miles (3.5 kilometers) to FS 529D, which drops off to the south to the House Creek road, FS 528. After this turnoff there is one more side trip on FS 529F at about 3.5 miles (5.5 kilometers), where it takes off

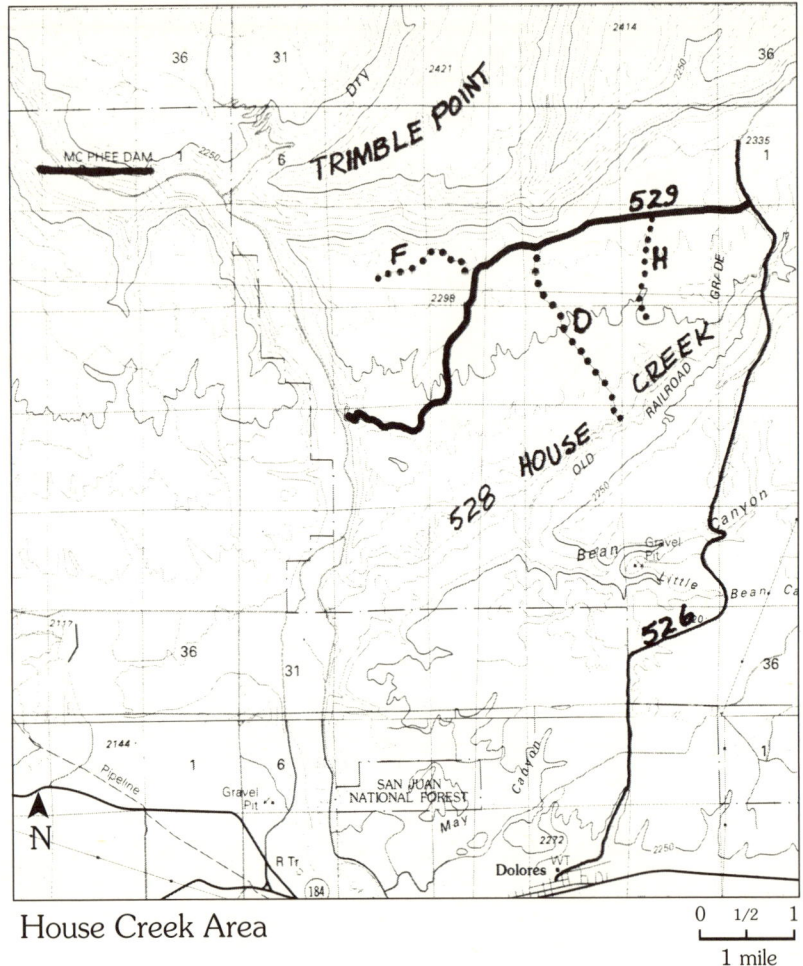

House Creek Area

to the right and ends at a point overlooking the reservoir. Some of the road is covered by loose silt that can make riding tedious.

From here it is about 2.2 miles (3.5 kilometers) of mostly descending road to the reservoir shore, which is rough and rocky from the waves produced by boats and wind pounding on the hill slopes.

Geology

Before reaching this ride, FS 526 drops off the House Creek fault escarpment that House Creek itself runs along. This fault is one of the major structures in the area but is inactive and will probably never rupture and release seismic energy. This fault is, however, an example of the regional trend of faults and fractures that influence the orientations of stream valleys and igneous intrusions (for instance, the sharp bends in the Dolores River and the east-west trend of the Hogback). This ride starts out on the Dakota Sandstone but drops down across the Morrison Formation, and along the shores of McPhee Reservoir, the white cliffs of Entrada Sandstone can be seen.

Dolores River Rides

The Dolores River valley east of Dolores, Colorado, is one of the most beautiful valleys anywhere. There are several rides described here that lead out directly from the main highway leading to Stoner and Rico (Colorado 145) and FS 535, which leads to Dunton up the West Dolores River. There is no trailhead for all of the trails, but camping is available at McPhee Reservoir or Forest Service campgrounds on FS 535, including Emerson, Mavreeso, and Goble.

A trip up the Dolores River valley between Dolores and Lizard Head Pass is recommended, and there are numerous roads and trails along the way. Many of the trails in this area are not very crowded with cyclists or hikers.

Bear Creek to Gold Run

Distance: 19 miles (30.5 kilometers) round trip

Difficulty: Moderate, but horse traffic creates technical sections

Quadrangle: Wallace Ranch, Orphan Butte, La Plata

Time: 3 to 5 hours

Tips: Be careful; watch for horse traffic and thunderheads on the western horizon

Elevation gain: 1,100 feet (335 meters)

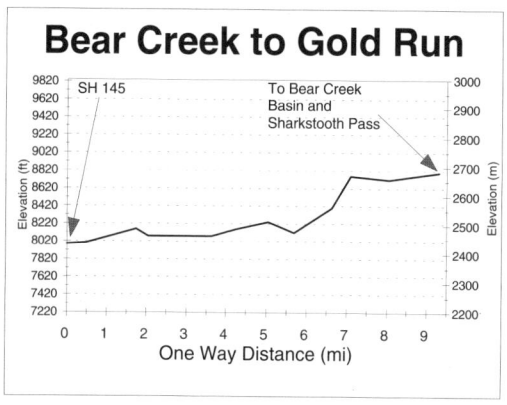

Description

The Bear Creek trailhead is located about 24 miles (38.5 kilometers) east of Dolores, Colorado, on Colorado 145. The trail takes off (elevation 7,898 feet; 2,407 meters) to the southeast and climbs up the Bear Creek valley for about 12 miles (19 kilometers), to where it joins the Sharkstooth Pass Trail and the Gold Run Trail. Much of the first ten miles is rideable and not terribly technical, though this area gets a lot of horse traffic, and many parts of the trail that enter the timber are rutted and roots are exposed, making riding difficult. The

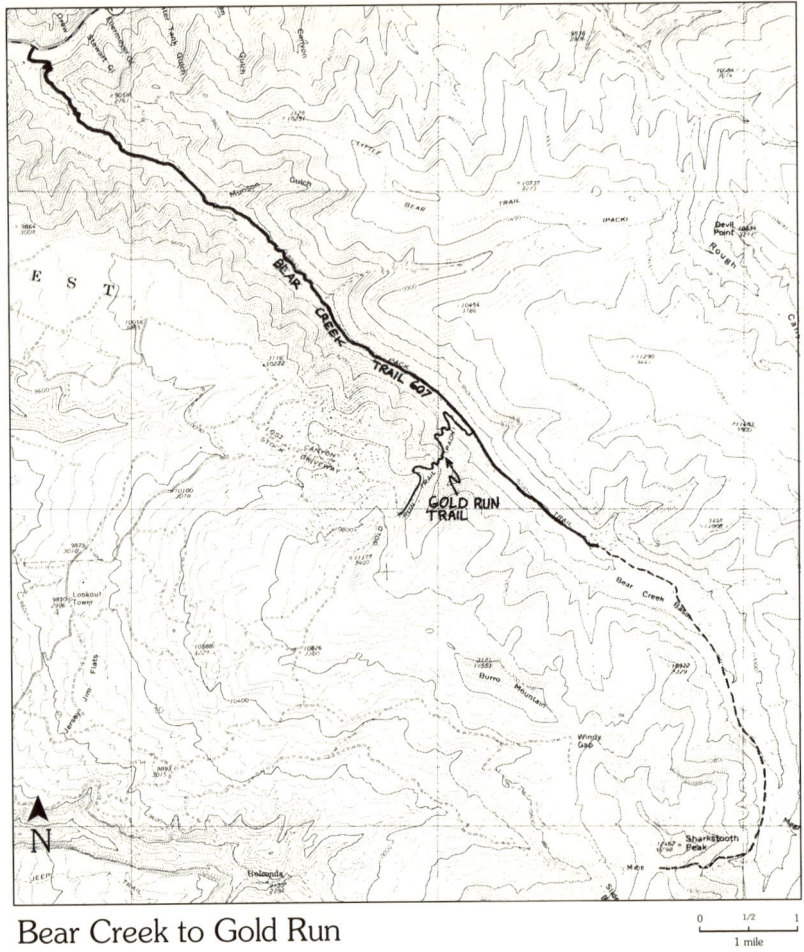

Bear Creek to Gold Run

horse traffic can also slow progress if there are many riders on the trail; stopping to yield to them is often required.

The Bear Creek valley is beautiful and lush and is recommended, if not for a mountain-bike trip, then for a hiking trip. This trail is also a good place to start a bicycle or backpacking trip that might end up in Mancos going over Sharkstooth Pass, Hesperus going through Cumberland Basin, or Durango going over Kenebec Pass. There are many side trails as well, such as Little Bear Trail and Gold Run Trail, both of which climb very steeply out of the canyon, though there is much better riding at the top.

Geology

This trail climbs gradually over alluvial bottom sediments through the stratigraphic column typical of the upper Dolores area, composed of, from bottom to top, the bright red Dolores Formation; the light tan, massive eolian (wind-deposited) Entrada/Junction Creek Sandstone; the slope-forming gray Morrison Formation; and the light gray caprock of Dakota Sandstone. There is little structure aside from the gentle westward dip of the formations.

# Stoner Mesa

Distance: 25.5 miles (41 kilometers) round trip
Difficulty: Hard
Quadrangle: Mancos
Time: 3 to 5 hours
Tips: Be careful; watch for traffic on the way up; serious descent at the end
Elevation gain: 2,444 feet (745 meters)

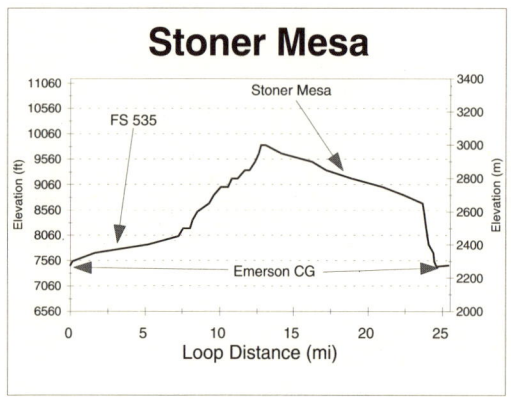

Description

Take Colorado 145 east out of Dolores for about 13 miles (21 kilometers) to the turnoff to the left on FS 535 to Dunton. This road follows the West Dolores River as it defines the southern limit of Stoner Mesa. The first Forest Service campground is Emerson, and this is the recommended start-finish. Park at the campground and ride back toward FS 535, turn right, and ride up the river for about 8

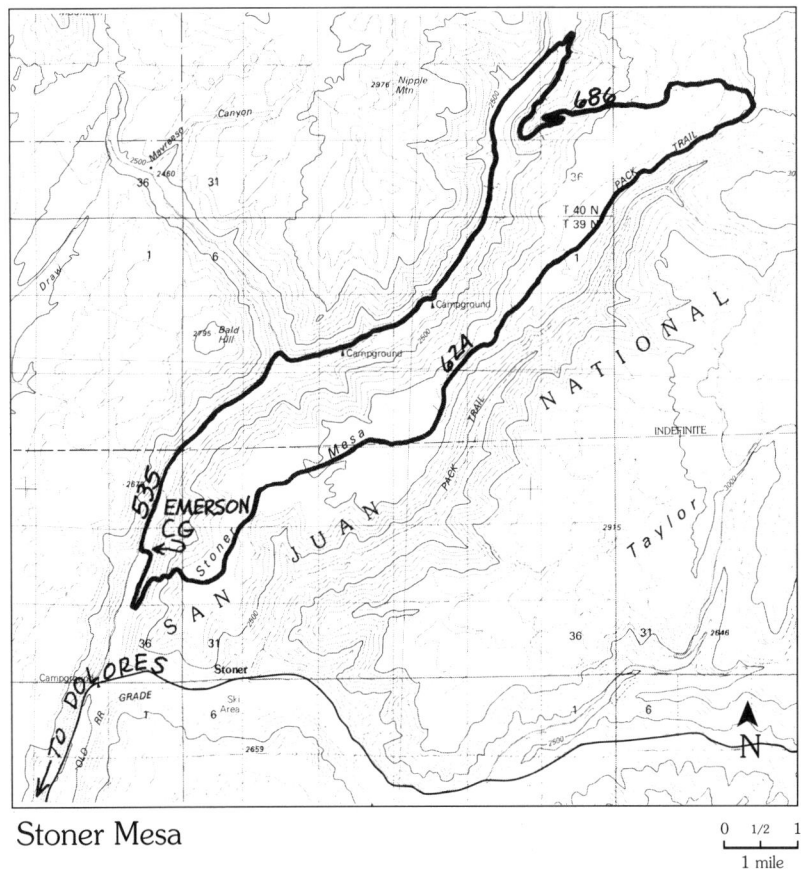

Stoner Mesa

miles (13 kilometers) to FS 686, which turns off to the right. Climb up out of the West Dolores River valley for about 7 miles (11.5 kilometers) to the Stoner Mesa trailhead (Trail 624), near Twin Springs. From here, the ride is predominantly downhill as it follows the top of Stoner Mesa southwest, and it is marked by posts in the open meadows. About 9 miles (14.5 kilometers) later, you begin a steep descent back to the river, dropping about 1,200 feet (370 meters) in about 2.5 miles (4 kilometers). The trail zigzags down the slope and is in pretty good shape after the first very steep 97 feet (30 meters), which can be intimidating. At the bottom, the trail meets a road, and turning right takes you across a bridge and back to Emerson Campground.

Geology

The ride begins in the Dolores Formation that outcrops along FS 535, then, as you climb up out of the valley you cross the Entrada Sandstone, Morrison Formation, and finally the Dakota Sandstone that caps Stoner Mesa, dipping gently to the southwest. From the mesa top, Lone Cone and Groundhog Mountain can be seen. These hills are the result of igneous intrusions much like the La Plata Mountains, but they were emplaced in late Tertiary time while the La Plata intrusives were close to the Cretaceous-Tertiary boundary.

Other Rides Around Mancos

The rides described so far most definitely do not reflect all of the mountain-bike opportunity in the Mancos area. There are several other very enjoyable rides south and west of the town, as well as on the roads around Mesa Verde National Park.

 # Weber Canyon

Distance: 7.5 miles (12 kilometers) round trip
Difficulty: Moderate
Quadrangle: Mancos, Trail Canyon
Time: 2 to 3
Tips: Be careful; uphill on way back; watch for traffic
Elevation gain: 500 feet (152 meters)

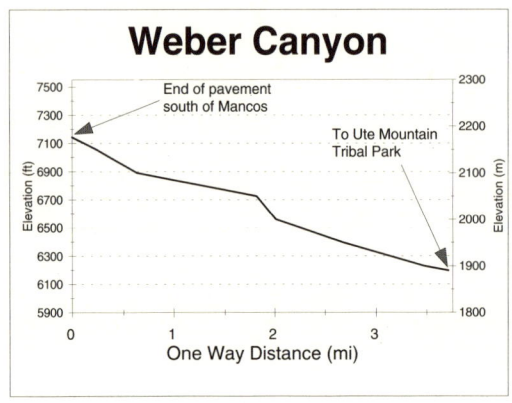

Description

Weber is pronounced locally as if it were spelled *Webber*. From the main intersection of U.S. 160 and Mancos's Main Street, head south through town, past Grand Avenue, and out onto the flat terrace of the Mancos River. Pavement ends two miles after leaving town, and two

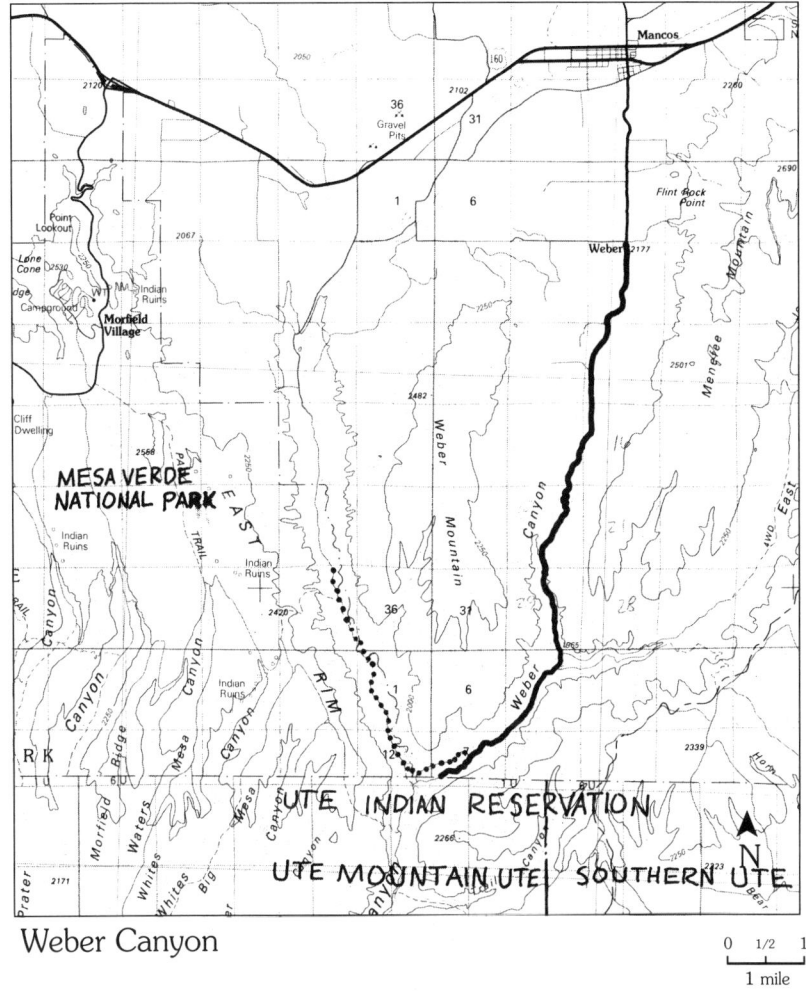

Weber Canyon

miles later the improved gravel road turns into an unimproved dirt road. There are several good hills with a few hundred feet of relief between the town and the dirt road, then the canyon drops continuously to the south for about four miles till access is stopped at the Southern Ute tribal property boundary. There are a few other trails that lead down into the valley and across the Mancos River, but few places are accessible and much of the land in the valley bottom is privately owned. All of the land to the east (Menefee Mountain) is owned by the Bureau of Land Management.

Biking in Weber Canyon.

Geology

The Weber road is situated on Mancos Shale, and the canyon walls above are composed of the overlying Mesa Verde Group. The prominent sandstone-forming cliffs on Menefee and Weber Mountains is the Point Lookout Sandstone, which is overlain by the coal-bearing Menefee Formation, and the highest prominence on Weber Mountain is composed of Cliff House Sandstone, named for the cliff dwellings built by Anasazi in Mesa Verde National Park.

Bibliography

Ellis, F. D. *Come Back to My Valley.* Cortez, Colo.: Cortez Printers, 1976.
Freeman, I. S. *A History of Montezuma County.* Boulder, Colo.: Johnson Publishing Company, 1958.
Haynes, D. D., J. D. Vogel, and D. G. Wyant. "Geology, Structure, and Uranium Deposits of the Cortez Quadrangle, Colorado and Utah." U.S. Geological Survey Miscellaneous Investigation Series Map I–629.
McTighe, J. *Roadside History of Colorado.* Boulder, Colo.: Johnson Publishing Company, 1984.
Petersen, K. L. "Climate and the Dolores River Anasazi: A Paleoenvironmental Reconstruction from a 10,000-Year Pollen Record, La Plata Mountains, Southwestern Colorado," in *Anthropological Papers.* Salt Lake City: University of Utah Press, 1988.
Smith, D. A. *Rocky Mountain Boom Town: A History of Durango.* Albuquerque: University of New Mexico Press, 1980.
Wenger, G. R. *The Story of Mesa Verde National Park.* Mesa Verde, Colo.: Mesa Verde Museum Association, 1980.

Index

Abajo Mountains, 13, 63
Àcoma, 3
Allard Mine, 96–97
Akin Reservoir, 59
Anasazi, 1–3, 8–9
Ancient Ones, 1
Animas River, 3
Animas-La Plata Water Project, 4

Babcock Peak, 98
Backcountry hazards and safety, 20–22
Bauer, George, 4
Bear, black, grizzly, 11
Bear Creek to Gold Run, 115–117
Bessie G Mine, 5, 108
Bike tools, 21
Biozones, 11
Boren Creek, 98–100
Box Canyon, 23
Burnt Ridge, 14, 72
Burro Mountain, 14
Burwell Peak, 98

Camp Bird Mine, 92
Cattle industry, La Plata Mountains area, 6, 22
Centennial Peak, 14
Cherry Creek, 80–81
Chicken Creek Road Loop, 50–51
Chicken Creek Trail, 45–47
Cliff dwellings, 1–3, 4, 8–9
Colorado Cliff Dwellings Association, 9
Colorado Federation of Women's Clubs, 9

Colorado Plateau, 13
Columbus Basin Mine, 5
Cooper, E. C., 7
Cortez, ix, 5
Coyote Park Loop, 66–69
Cumberland Basin, 93–95, 108–109
Cumberland Mine, 93, 108
Cutler Formation, 32, 95, 108

Dakota Sandstone, 13
Diorite, 14
Dolores (town of), ix
Dolores River Valley, 110, 114–120
Doyle Mine, 5, 84
Durango (town of), ix, 4–5, 8–9, 17–18
Durango Wheel Club, 17

Eagle Pass, 101–103
East Mancos River drainage, 77
East Mancos Trails, 78–79
Echo Basin Loop, 70–72
Entrada Sandstone, 32, 113
Escalante, Father, 3

Flooding. *See* Backcountry hazards and safety
Fort Lewis, 4, 91
Fossils, 13
Frink, George, 4

Geology, La Plata Mountains area, 13–15
Giles, Dick, 3–4
Glaciers, 14–15
Glaciers, rock, 15, 39–40, 74

Golconda, 5, 23, 33–36
Gold King Mill, 91, 93, 103
Gold Run Loop, 48–49
Graybeal Spring, 64–65
Graybeal, Wylie, 4, 64
Guyman Cabin, 73

Haycamp Point, 54–59
Henry Mountains, 13
Hermosa Creek, 95
Hesperus (town of), 4, 91
Hesperus Mountain, 14
Hogback, The, 73–75
Hohokam, 1
Hopi, 3
Horseback riding, 22
House Creek Area, 111–113
Hypothermia, 21

Ignacio (town of), 4
Igneous rocks, 13–14

Jackson, Captain George A., 5
Jackson City, 5
Jackson Gulch Reservoir, 24
Jersey Jim Loop, 26–28
Joe Moore Reservoir, 52
Junction Creek Sandstone, 78

Kenebec Pass, 93
Kroeger Campground, 91

La Plata Canyon, 91–92
La Sal Mountains, 13
Lewis Creek, 103
Lightner Creek, 93, 95
Lightning, hazards of, 20

Madden Peak, 77, 86–87
Mancos (town of), ix, 4
Mancos Hill, 6
Mancos River, 3
Mancos Shale, 13, 19–20, 39–40
Mancos Valley, ix, 3–5
Mancos State Recreation Area, 24, 47
Mayday, 91
McPhee Reservoir, 110
Menefee (family), 4, 6

Menefee Mountain, ix, 6, 88–90
Menefee Peak, 88–90
Mesa Verde National Park, 1, 8–9
Mesa Verde Group (geologic), 6, 13, 63, 90
Millwood, 7, 76
Mining, La Plata Mountains area, 5–6, 91–92
Mogollon, 1
Montezuma National Forest, 7
Montezuma Valley, 1
Monzonite, 14, 91
Morrison Formation, 13
Morrison Trail 610, 29–32
Moss, John, 3
Mountain lions. *See* Wildlife

Navajo Trail, ix
North Fork (West Mancos River drainage), 5, 37–40
North Star Mine, 5

Ohio Blue Tip Match Company, 8
Ott's Mill, 8

Paquin, Lou, 4
Parrott City, 5, 91
Pikes Peak Granite, 14
Point Lookout, 63
Point Lookout Sandstone, 63, 90, 124
Pueblo culture, 1–2

Railroads, Denver and Rio Grande, 4–5, 7
Railroad Grade, 80–81
Rampart Hills, 14, 60, 61–63
Ratliff, John, 3
Red Arrow Mine, 8
Reddert Ranch, 82
Rush Basin, 82–85
Rush, J. M., 5

Safety, outdoor. *See* Backcountry hazards
Salvero, Father, 3
San Juan Basin, 13
San Juan National Forest, 18

San Juan River, 91
Sangre de Cristo Mountains, 3
Savage Basin, 92
Silver Creek, 73
Silverton (town of), 5, 6
Slide Rock Basin, 15
Snowstorm Peak, 91, 108
Snowstorm Peak Loop, 107–109
Spiller Peak, 14, 77, 98
Spruce Lake, 51
Spruce Mill, 42
Spruce Mill Park, 7, 42–43
Spruce Water Canyon, 54, 58
Stoner Mesa, 118–120
Syenite, 14, 91

T-Down Corral, 60
Telluride (town of), 6

Thompson Park, 19
Timber industry, La Plata Mountains area, 7–8, 23
Tomahawk Mine, 104–106
Transfer Campground, 24–25, 47
Transfer to Millwood, 52–53

Ute, 3, 4, 92

Wade, John, 5
Weber Canyon, 122–124
West Mancos River drainage, 23
Wetherill (family), 8
Wildlife, La Plata Mountains area, 11–13
Windy Gap/Twin Lakes, 41–44

Zuni, 3